Better Homes and Gardens®

comfort
food
familydinners

Better Homes and Gardens®

comfort
food
family dinners

JG
PRESS

This book is printed on acid-free paper.

Copyright © 2010 by Meredith Corporation, Des Moines, IA. All rights reserved

Published by World Publications Group, Inc., 140 Laurel Street, East Bridgewater, MA 02333, www.wrldpub.net

Library of Congress Cataloging-in-Publication Data

Comfort food family dinners.
    p. cm.
  Cover title: At head of title: Better homes and gardens
  Includes index.
  ISBN 978-1-57215-625-8 (cloth) -- ISBN 978-1-57215-630-2 (pbk.)
  1. Dinners and dining. I. Better Homes and Gardens Books (Firm) II. Title: Better homes and gardens comfort food family dinners. III. Title: Better homes and gardens.
  TX737.C628 2010
  641.5'4--dc22

                                        2010019518

Printed in China.

10 9 8 7 6 5 4 3 2 1

Better Homes and Gardens®

Test Kitchen

Our seal assures you that every recipe in *Comfort Food Family Dinners* has been tested in the Better Homes and Gardens Test Kitchen®. This means that each recipe is practical and reliable and meets our high standards of taste appeal. We guarantee your satisfaction with this book for as long as you own it.

contents

appetizers

Marinated Shrimp Scampi, *recipe page 26*

fruit KABOBS

Kabobs are a fun way to serve fruit for parties, and a cool dip adds extra pizzazz. Seasonal substitutes, such as fresh peaches, nectarines, and plums or mangoes, add flavorful variety.

Prep: 20 minutes
Chill: 30 to 60 minutes
Makes: 8 servings (1 kabob and 2 tablespoons dip)

¾ cup cantaloupe chunks

¾ cup honeydew melon chunks

¾ cup small strawberries

¾ cup pineapple chunks

2 small bananas, peeled and cut into 1-inch slices

1 cup orange juice

¼ cup lime juice

1 8-ounce carton low-fat or fat-free vanilla yogurt

2 tablespoons frozen orange juice concentrate, thawed

Ground nutmeg or ground cinnamon (optional)

1 On eight 6-inch or four 10-inch skewers, alternately thread the cantaloupe, honeydew melon, strawberries, pineapple, and bananas. Place kabobs in a glass baking dish. Combine orange juice and lime juice; pour evenly over kabobs. Cover; chill kabobs for 30 to 60 minutes, turning occasionally.

2 Meanwhile, for dip, in a small bowl stir together the yogurt and orange juice concentrate. Cover and chill until ready to serve.

3 To serve, arrange the kabobs on a serving platter; discard juice mixture. If desired, sprinkle nutmeg or cinnamon over dip. Serve dip with kabobs.

Nutrition facts per serving: 91 cal.,1 g total fat (0 g sat. fat), 2 mg chol., 20 mg sodium, 21 g carbo., 1 g fiber, 2 g pro.

rosemary-seasoned NUTS

Satisfy a snack attack with a handful of these savory nibbles. They're terrific made with just one nut or a blend of all three.

Prep: 10 minutes
Bake: 15 minutes
Oven: 350°F
Makes: 12 (¼-cup) servings

Nonstick cooking spray

1 **egg white**

2 **teaspoons snipped fresh rosemary or 1 teaspoon dried rosemary, crushed**

½ **teaspoon salt**

½ **teaspoon coarsely ground black pepper**

3 **cups walnuts, hazelnuts (filberts), and/or whole almonds**

Fresh rosemary sprigs (optional)

1 Preheat oven to 350°F. Line a 13×9×2-inch baking pan with foil; lightly coat foil with nonstick cooking spray and set aside. In a medium bowl, beat egg white with a fork until frothy. Add snipped or dried rosemary, salt, and pepper, beating with the fork until combined. Add nuts; toss to coat.

2 Spread nut mixture in an even layer in the prepared pan. Bake for 15 to 20 minutes or until golden brown, stirring once.

3 Remove foil with nuts from pan; set aside to cool. Break up any large pieces. If desired, garnish with rosemary sprigs.

Nutrition facts per serving: 198 cal., 20 g total fat (2 g sat. fat), 0 mg chol., 102 mg sodium, 4 g carbo., 2 g fiber, 5 g pro.

three-herb DEVILED EGGS

These lunchtime favorites will be a star at dinnertime or at your next party. Chop up the leftover egg tops to use in a chef's salad or egg salad.

Start to Finish: 30 minutes
Makes: 6 servings

12 **hard-cooked eggs,* peeled**

¼ **cup mayonnaise or salad dressing**

¼ **cup dairy sour cream**

2 **to 3 teaspoons Dijon-style mustard**

2 **tablespoons snipped fresh parsley**

2 **tablespoons snipped fresh dill or 1½ teaspoons dried dill**

2 **tablespoons snipped fresh chives**

Sea salt or salt

Ground black pepper

Paprika or cayenne pepper (optional)

❶ Cut the top off each of the hard-cooked eggs about one-third from the top; scoop out yolk. Cut a small thin slice off the rounded bottom of each so it sits flat. If desired, chill tops for another use.

❷ Place yolks in a bowl; mash with a fork. Add mayonnaise, sour cream, and mustard; mix well. Stir in parsley, dill, and chives. Season to taste with salt and black pepper. Stuff egg yolk mixture into egg whites. If desired, sprinkle tops with paprika or cayenne pepper.

Nutrition facts per serving: 213 cal., 16 g total fat (5 g sat. fat), 430 mg chol., 305 mg sodium, 4 g carbo., 0 g fiber, 13 g pro.

*Test Kitchen Tip: To save time, purchase hard-cooked eggs at your supermarket's deli. Or cook the eggs ahead. To hard-cook eggs, place 12 eggs in a single layer in a large Dutch oven. Add just enough cold water to cover the eggs. Bring to a rapid boil over high heat. Remove from heat; cover and let stand for 15 minutes. Drain. Place eggs in ice water until cool enough to handle; drain. To peel, gently tap each egg on countertop. Roll egg between the palms of your hands. Peel off shell, starting at the large end. Cover and chill until ready to use (up to 24 hours).

crispy PARMESAN CHIPS

These homemade chips require no dip or spread since the cheese is baked right in. Look for wonton wrappers in the refrigerated area of the produce section.

Start to Finish: 30 minutes
Makes: 15 (4-chip) servings

30   **wonton wrappers**
    Nonstick cooking spray
 2   **tablespoons olive oil**
 1   **clove garlic, minced**
½   **teaspoon dried basil, crushed**
¼   **cup grated Parmesan or Romano cheese**

1 Preheat oven to 350°F. Use a sharp knife to cut wonton wrappers diagonally in half to form 60 triangles. Spray a baking sheet with nonstick coating. Arrange one-third of the triangles in a single layer on prepared baking sheet.

2 In a small bowl, stir together the olive oil, garlic, and basil. Brush the wonton triangles lightly with some of the oil mixture; sprinkle with some of the Parmesan or Romano cheese.

3 Bake for about 8 minutes or until golden brown. Cool completely on a wire rack. Repeat with the remaining wonton triangles, oil mixture, and Parmesan or Romano cheese.

Nutrition facts per serving: 70 cal., 3 g total fat (1 g sat. fat), 3 mg chol., 123 mg sodium, 9 g carbo., 0 g fiber, 2 g pro.

prosciutto-basil CHEESE BALL

Prep: 35 minutes
Chill: 4 hours
Stand: 15 minutes
Makes: 2 (1-cup) servings

1   8-ounce package cream
    cheese
4   ounces fontina cheese, finely
    shredded (1 cup)
¼   cup butter
1   tablespoon milk
½   teaspoon Worcestershire
    sauce for chicken
2   ounces prosciutto, chopped
2   tablespoons thinly sliced
    green onion
2   tablespoons snipped fresh
    basil
½   cup chopped toasted pine
    nuts
    Apples, assorted crackers,
    and/or flatbreads

1 In a large mixing bowl, let cream cheese, shredded cheese, and butter stand at room temperature for 30 minutes. Add milk and Worcestershire sauce. Beat with an electric mixer on medium speed until light and fluffy. Stir in prosciutto, green onion, and basil. Cover and chill for 4 to 24 hours.

2 Before serving, shape mixture into a ball. Roll ball in pine nuts and let stand for 15 minutes. Serve with apples, crackers, and/or flatbread.

Nutrition facts per 1 tablespoon spread: 63 cal., 6 g total fat (3 g sat. fat), 16 mg chol., 62 mg sodium, 1 g carbo., 0 g fiber, 2 g pro.

Make Ahead: Prepare as directed in step 1 and roll into a ball. Wrap cheese ball in moisture- and vapor-proof plastic wrap. Freeze for up to 1 month. To serve, thaw in refrigerator overnight. Unwrap and roll in nuts. Let stand for 15 minutes at room temperature before serving. To make logs: Divide mixture into four portions. Shape into 5-inch-long logs before rolling in nuts.

chèvre AND TOMATO SPREAD

Goat cheese, with its intense tangy flavor, is a delightful complement to dried tomatoes. Together, they make an ideal spread for entertaining or everyday snacking.

Prep: 20 minutes
Chill: 2 to 4 hours
Makes: 10 (1¼-cups) servings

⅓ cup dried tomatoes (not oil-packed)

4 ounces soft goat cheese (chèvre)

½ of an 8-ounce package reduced-fat cream cheese (Neufchâtel), softened

¼ cup snipped fresh basil or 2 teaspoons dried basil, crushed

3 cloves garlic, minced

⅛ teaspoon ground black pepper

1 to 2 tablespoons fat-free milk

10 slices party rye bread or 20 assorted reduced-fat crackers

Assorted garnishes, such as quartered cherry tomatoes, broccoli florets, chopped yellow sweet pepper, and/ or small fresh basil leaves (optional)

1 In a small bowl, cover dried tomatoes with boiling water. Let stand for 10 minutes. Drain tomatoes, discarding liquid. Finely snip tomatoes.

2 In a bowl, stir together the snipped tomatoes, goat cheese, cream cheese, basil, garlic, and black pepper. Stir in enough milk to make the mixture of spreading consistency. Cover and chill for 2 to 4 hours. Serve with rye bread or crackers. If desired, top with assorted garnishes.

Nutrition facts per 2 slices party rye and 2 tablespoons spread: 94 cal., 6 g total fat (3 g sat. fat), 19 mg chol., 202 mg sodium, 6 g carbo., 0 g fiber, 4 g pro.

artichoke-and-mushroom-topped CAMEMBERT

Start to Finish: 20 minutes
Makes: 6 servings

1 4½-ounce package
  Camembert or Brie cheese

1 6-ounce jar marinated
  artichokes

2 cups cremini or button
  mushrooms, quartered

¼ cup bottled roasted sweet
  red pepper, chopped

¼ cup finely shredded Parmesan
  cheese

12 ¼-inch-thick baguette slices,
  toasted*

1 Cut cheese into six wedges. Place one wedge on each of six small plates; set aside.

2 Drain artichoke hearts, reserving liquid. Cut artichokes into thin slivers; set aside. In a large skillet, heat reserved liquid. Add mushrooms; cook until tender. Stir in artichokes and roasted red pepper. Heat through.

3 Spoon mixture atop cheese wedges. Sprinkle with Parmesan cheese. Add two baguette slices to each plate. Serve at once.

Nutrition facts per serving: 142 cal., 8 g total fat (4 g sat. fat), 18 mg chol., 401 mg sodium, 11 g carbo., 1 g fiber, 8 g pro.

*To toast baguette slices: Preheat broiler. Place baguette slices on a baking sheet. Broil 2 to 3 inches from heat for 2 to 3 minutes or until light brown, turning once.

creamy SPINACH DIP

Dips typically are loaded with fat, but by combining fat-free cottage cheese and light mayo, you get all the creaminess of a traditional dip without the unwanted extra calories and fat.

Prep: 15 minutes
Chill: 1 to 4 hours
Makes: 8 (about 1¾-cups) servings

1½ cups fat-free cottage cheese

⅓ cup light mayonnaise dressing or salad dressing

1 tablespoon lemon juice

1 tablespoon fat-free milk

1 clove garlic, minced

½ teaspoon dried Italian seasoning, crushed

Pinch ground black pepper

1 cup finely chopped fresh spinach

Assorted vegetable dippers, such as carrot, celery, zucchini, or sweet pepper sticks; cucumber slices; and/ or cauliflower or broccoli florets

1 In a blender container or food processor bowl, combine the cottage cheese, mayonnaise dressing or salad dressing, lemon juice, milk, garlic, Italian seasoning, and pepper. Cover and blend or process until smooth. Stir in spinach. Cover and chill for 1 to 4 hours or overnight.

2 Stir dip before serving. Serve with vegetable dippers.

Nutrition facts per 1 carrot and 3 tablespoons dip: 98 cal., 4 g total fat (1 g sat. fat), 2 mg chol., 281 mg sodium, 11 g carbo., 2 g fiber, 6 g pro.

Skinnier Dairy Products

Fat-free milk (previously called skim) and reduced-fat milk (previously called low fat) have been around for years, but now almost every dairy-based product has a low-fat or fat-free version. Great news, since a low-fat diet is essential to controlling weight and minimizing health risks. Fat-free versions of yogurt, cottage cheese, and ice cream are readily available, and the majority of these dairy products have the full flavor we've come to expect. The next time you buy a dairy product, try the reduced-fat version or the fat-free version. You may be pleasantly surprised.

warm ARTICHOKE AND SALSA DIP

Suit your taste by selecting a green salsa with a heat level that you like.

Start to Finish: 15 minutes
Makes: 6 (¼-cup) servings

1   **12-ounce jar or two 6-ounce jars marinated artichoke hearts**

⅓   **cup sliced green onions**

2   **tablespoons bottled green salsa**

½   **cup shredded Monterey Jack or white cheddar cheese (2 ounces)**

¼   **cup dairy sour cream**

¼   **cup snipped fresh cilantro**

     Toasted baguette slices and/ or assorted crackers

1 Drain artichokes, discarding marinade. Coarsely chop artichokes. In a small saucepan, combine chopped artichokes, green onions, and salsa. Cook over medium heat until heated through, stirring frequently. Remove from heat. Stir in cheese, sour cream, and cilantro. Serve immediately with toasted baguette slices and/or assorted crackers.

Nutrition facts per serving: 144 cal., 13 g total fat (5 g sat. fat), 12 mg chol., 256 mg sodium, 5 g carbo., 0 g fiber, 3 g pro.

muffaletta SPREAD

Start to Finish: 20 minutes
Makes: 18 (2-tablespoon) servings

1¼ **cups pimiento-stuffed green olives**

1¼ **cups pitted kalamata olives**

3 **cloves garlic**

⅓ **cup olive oil**

2 **tablespoons red wine vinegar**

½ **cup finely chopped salami (2 ounces)**

½ **cup finely chopped capocolla or cooked ham (2 ounces)**

½ **cup shredded provolone cheese (2 ounces)**

2 **tablespoons snipped fresh parsley**

1 **teaspoon dried Italian seasoning, crushed**

¼ **teaspoon ground black pepper**

Assorted crackers or toasted baguette-style French bread slices

1 In a food processor, combine olives and garlic. Cover and process with three or four on-off turns or until finely chopped. With food processor running, slowly add olive oil and vinegar until nearly smooth. Transfer mixture to a medium bowl. Stir in salami, capocolla, cheese, parsley, Italian seasoning, and pepper. Serve immediately or cover and chill for up to 24 hours. Serve with crackers or toasted baguette slices.

Nutrition facts per serving: 100 cal., 10 g total fat (2 g sat. fat), 8 mg chol., 392 mg sodium, 2 g carbo., 1 g fiber, 2 g pro.

salmon-cucumber DIP

Cucumbers provide just the right amount of crunchy texture to this dip, which also can be used as a spread for making dainty tea sandwiches. The salmon makes this snack elegant enough to serve to party guests.

Prep: 20 minutes
Chill: 1 to 4 hours
Makes: 16 (about 2 cups) servings

1   **8-ounce carton fat-free dairy sour cream**

2   **tablespoons catsup or chili sauce**

1   **tablespoon finely chopped onion**

¼   **teaspoon salt**

½   **cup flaked, cooked salmon or canned salmon, drained, flaked, and skin and bones removed**

½   **cup finely chopped seeded cucumber**

1   **plum tomato, seeded and finely chopped**

1   **tablespoon snipped fresh dill or parsley**

   Whole grain crackers or assorted vegetable dippers

1 In a medium mixing bowl, combine sour cream, ketchup or chili sauce, onion, and salt. Stir in the salmon, cucumber, tomato, and dill or parsley. Cover and chill for 1 to 4 hours.

2 Serve dip with assorted crackers or vegetable dippers.

Nutrition facts per 4 crackers and 2 tablespoons dip: 86 cal., 3 g total fat (0 g sat. fat), 2 mg chol., 167 mg sodium, 11 g carbo., 3 g fiber, 3 g pro.

layered FIESTA SHRIMP DIP

Start to Finish: 20 minutes
Makes: about 4 cups

- 2 8-ounce packages cream cheese, softened
- 2 tablespoons mayonnaise or salad dressing
- 1 fresh jalapeño pepper, seeded and finely chopped*
- 2 cloves garlic, minced
- 1 cup bottled lime and garlic salsa or habanero-lime salsa
- 12 ounces fresh or frozen peeled, cooked shrimp, halved lengthwise
- 1 cup chopped mango
- 1 cup chopped, seeded roma tomatoes
- ¼ cup sliced green onions
- 2 tablespoons snipped fresh cilantro
- Tortilla chips

1 In a medium mixing bowl, beat cream cheese, mayonnaise, jalapeño, and garlic with an electric mixer on medium to high speed until creamy. Spread mixture on a 12-inch serving platter. Spread salsa over cream cheese layer to cover. Top with shrimp.

2 In a medium bowl, combine mango, tomato, green onions, and cilantro. Sprinkle mango mixture over shrimp. Serve immediately or cover and refrigerate for up to 4 hours. Serve with tortilla chips.

Nutrition facts per serving dip with chips: 221 cal., 15 g total fat (7 g sat. fat), 64 mg chol., 301 mg sodium, 14 g carbo., 1 g fiber, 8 g pro.

*Test Kitchen Tip: Because chile peppers contain volatile oils that can burn your skin and eyes, avoid direct contact with them as much as possible. When working with chile peppers, wear plastic or rubber gloves. If your bare hands do touch the peppers, wash your hands and nails well with soap and warm water.

spicy SPINACH-STUFFED MUSHROOMS

Prep: 30 minutes
Bake: 10 minutes
Oven: 425°F
Makes: 24 appetizers

24 large fresh button mushrooms (1½ to 2 inches in diameter)

2 tablespoons olive oil

Salt and ground black pepper

8 ounces spicy bulk Italian sausage

¼ cup finely chopped onion

¼ cup finely chopped red sweet pepper

1 clove garlic, minced

1 cup fresh spinach, chopped

¼ cup finely shredded Parmesan cheese

¼ cup fine dry bread crumbs

① Preheat oven to 425°F. Rinse and drain mushrooms. Remove stems; set aside. Brush mushroom caps with olive oil. Sprinkle with salt and pepper. Set aside.

② In a large skillet, cook chopped stems, sausage, onion, sweet pepper, and garlic over medium heat until sausage is brown. Stir in spinach until wilted. Stir in Parmesan cheese and bread crumbs. Remove from heat. Spoon sausage mixture into mushroom caps. Place on a greased baking sheet.

③ Bake for about 10 minutes or until stuffing is brown and mushrooms are tender.

Nutrition facts per appetizer: 57 cal., 5 g total fat (1 g sat. fat), 8 mg chol., 127 mg sodium, 2 g carbo., 0 g fiber, 2 g pro.

marinated SHRIMP SCAMPI

Prep: 35 minutes
Marinate: 1 hour
Broil: 4 minutes
Makes: 10 to 12 servings

2 **pounds fresh or frozen extra-jumbo shrimp in shells (30 to 40)**

¼ **cup olive oil**

¼ **cup dry white wine**

6 **cloves garlic, minced (1 tablespoon)**

2 **teaspoons finely shredded lemon peel**

½ **teaspoon crushed red pepper**

½ **teaspoon salt**

2 **tablespoons snipped fresh parsley**

❶ Thaw shrimp, if frozen. Peel and devein shrimp, leaving tails intact. Rinse shrimp; pat dry. Place shrimp in a large resealable plastic bag set in a shallow bowl.

❷ Combine olive oil, wine, garlic, lemon peel, crushed red pepper, and salt. Pour over shrimp. Seal bag; toss gently to coat. Marinate in refrigerator for 1 hour.

❸ Remove shrimp from marinade, reserving marinade. Arrange shrimp on unheated rack of a broiler pan. Broil 4 to 5 inches from heat for 2 minutes. Turn shrimp and brush with reserved marinade; broil for 2 to 4 minutes more or until shrimp are opaque. To serve, mound shrimp on platter; sprinkle with parsley.

Nutrition facts per serving: 126 cal., 4 g total fat (1 g sat. fat), 138 mg chol., 193 mg sodium, 2 g carbo., 1 g fiber, 19 g pro.

roasted PEPPER ROLL-UPS

The spinach and roasted red peppers combine for a bright, colorful filling. The high-fiber and high-protein beans create a very nutritious snack.

Prep: 20 minutes
Chill: 2 to 24 hours
Makes: 6 servings

- 1 **15-ounce can white kidney (cannellini) beans, rinsed and drained**
- ½ **of an 8-ounce package reduced-fat cream cheese (Neufchâtel), softened**
- ¼ **cup packed fresh basil**
- 1 **tablespoon fat-free milk**
- 2 **small cloves garlic, quartered**
- ⅛ **teaspoon ground black pepper**
- ⅓ **cup roasted red sweet peppers, drained and finely chopped**
- 6 **6-inch flour tortillas**
- 1 **cup packed spinach leaves**

1 For the filling, in a blender container or food processor bowl combine the beans, cream cheese, basil, milk, garlic, and black pepper. Cover and blend or process until smooth. Stir in roasted sweet peppers.

2 To assemble, spread about ⅓ cup of the filling evenly over each tortilla to within ½ inch of the edges. Arrange spinach leaves over filling to cover. Carefully roll tortillas up tightly. Cover and chill roll-ups for 2 to 24 hours.

3 To serve, use a sharp knife to cut roll-ups crosswise into 1½-inch slices. Serve immediately.

Nutrition facts per serving: 173 cal., 7 g total fat (3 g sat. fat), 15 mg chol., 289 mg sodium, 24 g carbo., 4 g fiber, 8 g pro.

nutty CUCUMBER SANDWICH

Select soft goat cheese that has been rolled in cracked black pepper to add another flavor dimension to this meatless sandwich.

Start to Finish: 15 minutes
Makes: 4 sandwiches

½ cup fresh snow pea pods, trimmed

½ of a medium cucumber

8 thin slices rye bread

3 to 4 ounces soft goat cheese (chèvre)

⅓ cup seasoned roasted soy nuts (such as ranch or garlic)

1 medium tomato, thinly sliced

Salt

1 In a covered small saucepan, cook the pea pods in a small amount of boiling lightly salted water for 2 minutes. Drain; rinse pea pods with cold water. Drain again. Place pea pods in a small bowl; chill until needed.

2 Use a vegetable peeler to remove a few lengthwise strips of peel from the cucumber. Thinly slice cucumber.

3 Spread one side of each bread slice with goat cheese. Sprinkle four of the bread slices with soy nuts, gently pressing nuts into the cheese. Top soy nuts with cucumber slices, tomato slices, and pea pods. Sprinkle with salt. Top with remaining bread slices, cheese sides down.

Nutrition facts per sandwich: 276 cal., 9 g total fat (4 g sat. fat), 10 mg chol., 540 mg sodium, 36 g carbo., 6 g fiber, 14 g pro.

mini SPINACH POCKETS

A savory spinach and onion mixture fills these miniature stuffed pizzas. The refrigerated pizza dough makes them incredibly easy to prepare.

Prep: 30 minutes
Bake: 8 minutes
Stand: 5 minutes
Oven: 425°F
Makes: 25 pockets

Nonstick cooking spray

½ **of a 10-ounce package frozen chopped spinach, thawed and well drained**

½ **of an 8-ounce package reduced-fat cream cheese (Neufchâtel), softened**

2 **tablespoons finely chopped green onion**

1 **tablespoon grated Parmesan cheese**

Pinch ground black pepper

1 **10-ounce package refrigerated pizza dough**

1 **tablespoon milk**

Bottled spaghetti sauce, warmed (optional)

1 Preheat oven to 425°F. Line a baking sheet with foil; lightly coat foil with nonstick cooking spray. Set baking sheet aside. For filling, in a medium bowl stir together spinach, cream cheese, green onion, Parmesan cheese, and pepper. Set aside.

2 Unroll pizza dough on a lightly floured surface; roll dough into a 15-inch square. Cut into twenty-five 3-inch squares. Spoon 1 rounded teaspoon filling onto each square. Brush edges of dough with water. Lift a corner of each square and stretch dough over filling to opposite corner, making a triangle. Press edges with fingers or a fork to seal.

3 Arrange pockets on the prepared baking sheet. Prick tops of pockets with a fork. Brush with milk. Bake for 8 to 10 minutes or until golden brown. Let stand for 5 minutes before serving. If desired, serve with spaghetti sauce.

Nutrition facts per pocket: 38 cal., 2 g total fat (1 g sat. fat), 4 mg chol., 62 mg sodium, 5 g carbo., 0 g fiber, 1 g pro.

Nutritional Powerhouse

Popeye may have eaten spinach to make him strong, but the leafy green veggie does a lot more than that. With only about 25 calories in a half pound, spinach is one of the most nutrient-dense vegetables around. That same half pound also contains a whopping 21 grams of fiber as well as more than three times the recommended daily amount of vitamin A and the phytochemicals lutein and indoles, which can help lower one's risk of cancer and maintain healthy vision.

turkey SALAD TARTLETS

Start to Finish: 25 minutes
Makes: 30 tartlets

1¼ cups chopped cooked turkey
    breast

3 slices packaged ready-to-serve
    cooked bacon, chopped, or
    3 slices bacon, crisp-cooked,
    drained, and crumbled

2 tablespoons finely chopped
    onion

2 tablespoons mayonnaise

2 tablespoons dairy sour cream

2 teaspoons lime juice

1 teaspoon Dijon-style mustard
    Salt
    Ground black pepper

1 avocado, halved, pitted,
    peeled, and chopped

2 2.1-ounce packages baked
    miniature phyllo dough
    shells (30 shells)

8 grape tomatoes, quartered
    lengthwise

1 In a medium bowl, combine turkey, bacon, and onion.

2 In a small bowl, stir together mayonnaise, sour cream, lime juice, mustard, and salt and pepper to taste. Add mayonnaise mixture to turkey mixture, stirring to combine.

3 Add avocado to turkey salad, gently tossing to combine. Spoon turkey salad into phyllo shells. Garnish tartlets with tomato wedges.

Nutrition facts per tartlet: 52 cal., 3 g total fat (0 g sat. fat), 6 mg chol., 38 mg sodium, 3 g carbo., 0 g fiber, 3 g pro.

Make Ahead: Prepare turkey salad through step 2. Cover and chill for up to 24 hours. Just before serving, stir in avocado and spoon salad into tart shells.

nutty CHICKEN FINGERS

A satisfying snack is ready in a jiffy when you make these crunchy coated chicken strips.

Prep: 15 minutes
Bake: 7 minutes
Oven: 400°F
Makes: 3 servings

⅓ **cup crushed cornflakes**

½ **cup finely chopped pecans**

1 **tablespoon dried parsley flakes**

⅛ **teaspoon salt**

⅛ **teaspoon garlic powder**

12 **ounces skinless, boneless chicken breasts, cut into 3x1-inch strips**

2 **tablespoons fat-free milk**

Reduced-calorie ranch-style dressing (optional)

1 Preheat oven to 400°F. In a shallow dish, combine crushed cornflakes, pecans, parsley, salt, and garlic powder. Dip chicken in milk, then roll in cornflake mixture. Place in a 15x10x1-inch baking pan.

2 Bake for 7 to 9 minutes or until chicken is tender and no longer pink. If desired, serve chicken with ranch-style dressing.

Nutrition facts per serving: 279 cal., 15 g total fat (0 g sat. fat), 66 mg chol., 219 mg sodium, 8 g carbo., 2 g fiber, 29 g pro.

black BEAN NACHOS

Prep: 20 minutes
Bake: 23 minutes
Oven: 350°F
Makes: 12 servings

6   7- or 8-inch flour tortillas
    Nonstick cooking spray
2   teaspoons taco seasoning mix
2   cups shredded Monterey
    Jack cheese or Colby and
    Monterey Jack cheese or
    Monterey Jack cheese with
    jalapeño chile peppers
    (8 ounces)
¾   cup canned black beans,
    rinsed and drained
¾   cup bottled thick and chunky
    salsa
½   cup loose-pack frozen whole
    kernel corn
    Dairy sour cream (optional)
    Snipped fresh cilantro
    (optional)

1 Preheat oven to 350°F. Cut each tortilla into eight wedges. Place half of the tortilla wedges in a single layer on a large baking sheet. Lightly coat with nonstick cooking spray; sprinkle with half of the taco seasoning mix. Bake for 8 to 10 minutes or until dry and crisp; cool. Repeat with remaining tortilla wedges and taco seasoning mix.

2 Mound chips on an 11- or 12-inch ovenproof platter or large baking sheet. Sprinkle with cheese. Bake for 5 to 7 minutes more or until cheese melts.

3 Meanwhile, in a small saucepan, combine beans, salsa, and corn. Cook over medium heat until heated through, stirring occasionally.

4 To serve, spoon bean mixture over the cheese-topped chips. If desired, top with sour cream and sprinkle with cilantro.

Nutrition facts per serving: 137 cal., 7 g total fat (4 g sat. fat), 17 mg chol., 338 mg sodium, 12 g carbo., 1 g fiber, 7 g pro.

artichoke-feta TORTILLAS

Three cheeses, roasted peppers, and artichokes melt and mingle in these tortilla-wrapped treats. They're the perfect appetizer for a casual gathering.

Prep: 15 minutes
Bake: 15 minutes
Oven: 350°F
Makes: 24 servings

Nonstick cooking spray

1 **14-ounce can artichoke hearts, drained and finely chopped**

½ **of an 8-ounce tub reduced-fat cream cheese (about ½ cup)**

3 **green onions, thinly sliced**

⅓ **cup grated Parmesan or Romano cheese**

¼ **cup crumbled feta cheese (1 ounce)**

3 **tablespoons reduced-fat basil pesto**

8 **8-inch spinach, tomato, or plain flour tortillas**

1 **7-ounce jar roasted red sweet peppers, drained and cut into strips**

Yogurt-Chive Sauce*

1 Preheat oven to 350°F. Lightly coat a 3-quart rectangular baking dish with nonstick cooking spray; set aside. For filling, in a large bowl stir together artichoke hearts, cream cheese, green onions, Parmesan cheese, feta cheese, and pesto.

2 Place about ¼ cup filling on each tortilla. Top with red pepper strips; roll up. Arrange tortilla rolls in the prepared baking dish. If desired, lightly coat tortilla rolls with additional cooking spray. Bake, uncovered, for about 15 minutes or until heated through.

3 Cut each tortilla roll into thirds and arrange on a serving platter. Serve with Yogurt-Chive Sauce.

***Yogurt-Chive Sauce:** In a small bowl, stir together one 8-ounce carton plain fat-free yogurt and 1 tablespoon snipped fresh chives.

Nutrition facts per serving: 75 cal., 4 g total fat (2 g sat. fat), 8 mg chol., 177 mg sodium, 8 g carbo., 1 g fiber, 3 g pro.

incredible QUESADILLAS

Capture a south-of-the-border attitude with these flavorful snacks. Cooking becomes a fun activity when you show the kids how to use a waffle baker.

Prep: 20 minutes
Cook: 3 minutes each
Makes: 8 servings

½ **cup shredded reduced-fat Mexican-cheese blend**

4 **8-inch fat-free flour tortillas**

4 **low-fat brown-and-serve sausage links, cooked and coarsely chopped**

2 **tablespoons well-drained pineapple salsa or tomato salsa**

1 **small red onion, sliced and separated into rings**

2 **tablespoons finely snipped fresh cilantro**

½ **cup pineapple salsa or tomato salsa**

Cilantro sprigs (optional)

1 Heat a waffle baker on a medium-high heat setting. Sprinkle 2 tablespoons of the cheese over half of each tortilla. Top with sausage, the 2 tablespoons salsa, onion, and cilantro. Fold tortillas in half, pressing gently.

2 Place one quesadilla on preheated waffle baker. Close lid, pressing slightly. Bake for 3 to 6 minutes or until tortilla is lightly browned and cheese is melted. Remove from waffle baker. Cut quesadilla in half. Repeat with remaining quesadillas.

3 Place the ½ cup salsa in a bowl. If desired, garnish quesadilla pieces with cilantro sprigs. Serve with salsa.

Note: Or cook each quesadilla in a 10-inch nonstick skillet over medium heat for 3 to 4 minutes or until golden brown. Using a spatula, turn quesadilla over. Cook for 2 to 3 minutes more or until golden brown. Remove the quesadilla from the skillet.

Nutrition facts per serving: 104 cal., 2 g total fat (1 g sat. fat), 8 mg chol., 362 mg sodium, 17 g carbo., 2 g fiber, 5 g pro.

soups
AND STEWS

Chunky Chipotle Pork Chili, *recipe page 58*

vegetable BARLEY SOUP

Barley has been nourishing folks for thousands of years. This pearl of a grain is so packed with protein that it makes this meatless soup hearty enough to serve as a main dish.

Prep: 15 minutes
Cook: 25 minutes
Makes: 5 (1¾-cup) servings

- 1 **14.5-ounce can reduced-sodium chicken broth**
- 1 **14.5-ounce can low-sodium tomatoes, undrained and cut up**
- 1 **cup chopped onion**
- ¾ **cup vegetable juice**
- ½ **cup quick-cooking barley**
- ½ **cup sliced celery**
- ½ **cup sliced carrot**
- 1 **tablespoon snipped fresh basil or 1 teaspoon dried basil, crushed**
- 1½ **teaspoons snipped fresh marjoram or ½ teaspoon dried marjoram, crushed**
- 2 **cloves garlic, minced**
- ¼ **teaspoon ground black pepper**
- 1 **medium yellow summer squash, cut into ¼-inch slices**
- 1 **9-ounce package frozen cut green beans**

1 In a large saucepan, stir together the chicken broth, undrained tomatoes, onion, vegetable juice, barley, celery, carrot, dried basil (if using), dried marjoram (if using), garlic, and pepper. Bring to boiling; reduce heat. Simmer, covered, for 20 minutes.

2 Stir in the squash, green beans, fresh basil (if using), and fresh marjoram (if using). Return mixture to boiling. Simmer, covered, for 5 to 10 minutes more or until vegetables are tender.

Nutrition facts per serving: 173 cal., 2 g total fat (0 g sat. fat), 0 mg chol., 480 mg sodium, 36 g carbo., 5 g fiber, 7 g pro.

vegetable PASTA SOUP

Start to Finish: 35 minutes
Makes: 6 servings

- 6 **cloves garlic, minced**
- 2 **teaspoons olive oil**
- 1½ **cups coarsely shredded carrots**
- 1 **cup chopped onion (1 large)**
- 1 **cup thinly sliced celery (2 stalks)**
- 1 **32-ounce box reduced-sodium chicken broth**
- 4 **cups water**
- 1½ **cups dried ditalini**
- ¼ **cup shaved Parmesan cheese**
- 2 **tablespoons snipped fresh parsley**

1 In a 5- to 6-quart Dutch oven, cook garlic in hot oil over medium heat for 15 seconds. Add carrots, onion, and celery; cook for 5 to 7 minutes or until tender, stirring occasionally. Add chicken broth and the water; bring to boiling. Add pasta; cook, uncovered, for 7 to 8 minutes or until pasta is tender.

2 To serve, top individual servings with Parmesan cheese and parsley.

Nutrition facts per serving: 172 cal., 4 g total fat (0 g sat. fat), 2 mg chol., 454 mg sodium, 28 g carbo., 2 g fiber, 8 g pro.

five-spice CHICKEN NOODLE SOUP

Asian dishes abound with flavor-packed ingredients. This soup is no exception, with its highlights of soy, five-spice powder, and ginger. All add a flavor punch without adding lots of calories or fat.

Start to Finish: 20 minutes
Makes: 4 (1½-cup) servings

2½ **cups water**

1¼ **cups reduced-sodium chicken broth**

2 **green onions, thinly bias-sliced**

2 **teaspoons reduced-sodium soy sauce**

2 **cloves garlic, minced**

¼ **teaspoon five-spice powder**

⅛ **teaspoon ground ginger**

2 **cups chopped bok choy**

1 **medium red sweet pepper, thinly sliced into strips**

2 **ounces dried somen noodles, broken into 2-inch lengths, or 2 ounces dried fine noodles**

1½ **cups chopped cooked chicken**

1 In a large saucepan, combine water, chicken broth, green onions, soy sauce, garlic, five-spice powder, and ginger. Bring to boiling. Stir in bok choy, sweet pepper strips, and noodles. Return to boiling; reduce heat. Boil gently, uncovered, for 3 to 5 minutes or until noodles are just tender. Stir in the cooked chicken. Heat through.

Nutrition facts per serving: 181 cal., 4 g total fat (1 g sat. fat), 51 mg chol., 556 mg sodium, 14 g carbo., 1 g fiber, 20 g pro.

turkey AND RICE SOUP

Serve crispy breadsticks with this meal-in-a-bowl.

Start to Finish: 25 minutes
Makes: 6 servings

2 14-ounce cans reduced-sodium chicken broth

1½ cups water

1 teaspoon snipped fresh rosemary or ¼ teaspoon dried rosemary, crushed

¼ teaspoon ground black pepper

1 medium carrot, thinly sliced

1 stalk celery, thinly sliced

1 small onion, thinly sliced

1 cup quick-cooking rice

½ cup frozen loose-pack cut green beans

2 cups chopped cooked turkey or chicken (about 10 ounces)

1 14.5-ounce can diced tomatoes, undrained

Fresh rosemary sprigs (optional)

1 In a large saucepan, combine broth, the water, snipped or dried rosemary, and pepper. Add carrot, celery, and onion. Bring to boiling.

2 Stir in uncooked rice and green beans. Return to boiling; reduce heat. Cover and simmer for 10 to 12 minutes or until vegetables are tender. Stir in turkey and undrained tomatoes; heat through. If desired, garnish with rosemary sprigs.

Nutrition facts per serving: 177 cal., 2 g total fat (1 g sat. fat), 35 mg chol., 500 mg sodium, 20 g carbo., 1 g fiber, 17 g pro.

tomato-tortellini SOUP

Start to Finish: 15 minutes
Makes: 4 servings

- 2 14-ounce cans reduced-sodium chicken broth or vegetable broth
- 1 9-ounce package refrigerated tortellini
- ½ of an 8-ounce tub cream cheese spread with chive and onion
- 1 10.75- or 11-ounce can condensed tomato or tomato bisque soup
  Snipped fresh chives (optional)

1 In a medium saucepan, bring broth to boiling. Add tortellini; reduce heat. Simmer, uncovered, for 5 minutes. In a bowl, whisk ⅓ cup of the hot broth into the cream cheese spread until smooth. Return all to saucepan along with tomato soup; heat through. If desired, sprinkle with chives.

Nutrition facts per serving: 363 cal., 14 g total fat (8 g sat. fat), 57 mg chol., 1,264 mg sodium, 44 g carbo., 1 g fiber, 14 g pro.

sausage AND GREENS RAGOÛT

Look in your supermarket's produce section for washed, packaged escarole, Swiss chard, kale, or spinach.

Start to Finish: 35 minutes
Makes: 4 servings

1 **8-ounce package cooked chicken andouille sausage links or cooked smoked turkey sausage links, cut into ½-inch slices**

1 **medium yellow summer squash, cut into ½-inch pieces**

1 **14-ounce can reduced-sodium chicken broth**

1 **tablespoon snipped fresh rosemary or 1 teaspoon dried rosemary, crushed**

2 **cups coarsely chopped fresh escarole, Swiss chard, baby kale, and/or spinach leaves**

1 **15-ounce can white kidney beans (cannellini beans), rinsed and drained**

1 **cup carrots cut into thin, bite-size sticks**

Ground black pepper

Purchased garlic croutons (optional)

1 In a large saucepan, combine sausage, squash, broth, and rosemary. Bring to boiling; reduce heat. Simmer, uncovered, for 5 minutes. Stir in escarole, beans, and carrots. Return to boiling; reduce heat. Cover and simmer for about 5 minutes more or until vegetables are tender. Season to taste with pepper. If desired, top each serving with croutons.

Nutrition facts per serving: 156 cal., 8 g total fat (2 g sat. fat), 20 mg chol., 785 mg sodium, 20 g carbo., 7 g fiber, 16 g pro.

sausage AND PEPPERS SOUP

Serve this soup on a cold and wintry day. It's hearty, it's healthy, it's spicy—and best of all, it's Italian. Did we mention that it can be made in under 30 minutes?

Prep: 10 minutes
Cook: 15 minutes
Makes: 4 (1½-cup) servings

¼ **pound bulk hot Italian turkey sausage**

1 **small green sweet pepper, thinly sliced**

1 **small yellow sweet pepper, thinly sliced**

1 **medium onion, cut into thin wedges**

2 **cloves garlic, minced**

1 **14.5-ounce can reduced-sodium chicken broth**

1¾ **cups water**

1 **14.5-ounce can low-sodium tomatoes, undrained and cut up**

1½ **cups cubed potatoes**

1 **tablespoon snipped fresh basil or 1 teaspoon dried basil, crushed**

¼ **teaspoon crushed red pepper (optional)**

❶ In a large saucepan, cook and stir sausage, sweet peppers, onion, and garlic over medium heat for about 5 minutes or until sausage is browned. Drain off fat.

❷ Stir in broth, water, undrained tomatoes, potatoes, and dried basil (if using). Bring to boiling; reduce heat. Simmer, covered, for 10 to 15 minutes or until potatoes are just tender. Stir in the fresh basil (if using), and, if desired, the crushed red pepper.

Nutrition facts per serving: 146 cal., 4 g total fat (1 g sat. fat), 21 mg chol., 472 mg sodium, 21 g carbo., 2 g fiber, 8 g pro.

Broth Basics

Although there is no Recommended Daily Allowance set for sodium, a daily limit of 2,400 mg of sodium is commonly suggested. A comparison of three chicken broth products illustrates the difference in the sodium content of each (note: brands will vary). All are based on 1 cup chicken broth:

Low sodium:	54 mg
Reduced sodium:	620 mg*
Regular:	985 mg
1 bouillon cube:	900 to 1,000 mg

*Due to better flavor, reduced-sodium broth rather than low-sodium broth is generally used in recipes in this book.

italian MEATBALL SOUP

Go Italian with this family-pleasing soup, as easy to make as it is hearty. Another day, partner the second half of the bag of frozen meatballs with prepared pasta sauce for a classic spaghetti-and-meatballs dinner.

Start to Finish: 25 minutes
Makes: 4 servings

- 1 **14.5-ounce can diced tomatoes with onion and garlic, undrained**
- 1 **14-ounce can reduced-sodium beef broth**
- 1½ **cups water**
- ½ **teaspoon dried Italian seasoning, crushed**
- ½ **of a 16-ounce package frozen Italian-style cooked meatballs**
- ½ **cup small dried pasta (such as ditalini or orzo)**
- 1 **cup frozen loose-pack mixed vegetables**
- 1 **tablespoon shredded or grated Parmesan cheese (optional)**

1 In a large saucepan, stir together undrained tomatoes, beef broth, water, and Italian seasoning. Bring to boiling. Add meatballs, pasta, and frozen vegetables. Return to boiling; reduce heat. Cover and simmer for about 10 minutes or until pasta and vegetables are tender. If desired, sprinkle individual servings with cheese.

Nutrition facts per serving: 275 cal., 13 g total fat (6 g sat. fat), 37 mg chol., 1,113 mg sodium, 25 g carbo., 4 g fiber, 15 g pro.

shrimp GAZPACHO

Gazpacho—a Spanish soup with tomatoes and onions—traditionally is served cold. We've made this gazpacho into a complete meal by adding succulent shrimp for a zingy thrill of a chill.

Prep: 35 minutes
Chill: 4 to 24 hours
Makes: 6 (1½-cup) servings

8 **medium ripe tomatoes, peeled, if desired, and chopped (2½ pounds)**

1 **medium cucumber, chopped**

1 **medium green or red sweet pepper, seeded and chopped**

¾ **cup low-sodium vegetable juice or low-sodium tomato juice**

½ **cup clam juice**

¼ **cup chopped onion**

3 **tablespoons red wine vinegar**

2 **tablespoons snipped fresh cilantro**

2 **tablespoons olive oil**

1 **clove garlic, minced**

¼ **teaspoon ground cumin**

1 **8-ounce package frozen, peeled, cooked small shrimp, thawed**

Fat-free dairy sour cream (optional)

1 In a large mixing bowl, combine tomatoes, cucumber, sweet pepper, vegetable juice or tomato juice, clam juice, onion, vinegar, cilantro, olive oil, garlic, and cumin. Gently fold the shrimp into the tomato mixture.

2 Cover and chill for 4 to 24 hours to allow flavors to blend. To serve, ladle into serving bowls. If desired, top each with a spoonful of sour cream.

Nutrition facts per serving: 141 cal., 6 g total fat (1 g sat. fat), 74 mg chol., 154 mg sodium, 15 g carbo., 4 g fiber, 11 g pro.

seafood AND CORN CHOWDER

Prep: 15 minutes
Cook: 20 minutes
Makes: 4 or 5 servings

1 **14-ounce can chicken broth**

1 **cup sliced celery (2 stalks)**

1 **cup chopped onion (1 large)**

½ **cup sliced carrot (1 medium)**

1 **14.75-ounce can cream-style corn**

1 **cup whipping cream**

½ **teaspoon snipped fresh thyme**

⅛ **teaspoon ground black pepper**

Few dashes bottled hot pepper sauce

10 **to 12 ounces cooked or canned lump crabmeat and/ or peeled, deveined cooked shrimp**

1 In a medium saucepan, combine broth, celery, onion, and carrot. Bring to boiling; reduce heat. Simmer, covered, for about 20 minutes or until vegetables are tender. Set aside; cool slightly.

2 Transfer half of the mixture to a blender or food processor. Cover and blend or process until smooth. Repeat with remaining mixture. Return mixture to saucepan. Stir in corn, whipping cream, thyme, black pepper, and hot pepper sauce. Bring to boiling; reduce heat. Stir in crabmeat and/or shrimp; heat through.

Nutrition facts per serving: 388 cal., 24 g total fat (14 g sat. fat), 154 mg chol., 948 mg sodium, 27 g carbo., 3 g fiber, 18 g pro.

spicy SEAFOOD STEW

Health experts recommend eating at least one meal per week that includes fish—let it be this one. Boneless fish fillets and whole shrimp simmer with garlic, herbs, and Cajun spices in a bayou blockbuster of a stew.

Prep: 15 minutes
Cook: 25 minutes
Makes: 4 (1⅓-cup) servings

8 ounces fresh or frozen skinless fish fillets (halibut, orange roughy, or sea bass)

6 ounces fresh or frozen peeled and deveined shrimp

2 teaspoons olive oil

⅔ cup chopped onion

½ cup finely chopped carrot

½ cup chopped red or green sweet pepper

2 cloves garlic, minced

1 14.5-ounce can low-sodium tomatoes, undrained and cut up

1 8-ounce can low-sodium tomato sauce

1 cup reduced-sodium chicken broth

¼ cup dry red wine or reduced-sodium chicken broth

2 bay leaves

1 tablespoon snipped fresh thyme or 1 teaspoon dried thyme, crushed

½ teaspoon Cajun seasoning

¼ teaspoon ground cumin

¼ teaspoon crushed red pepper (optional)

1 Thaw fish and shrimp, if frozen. Rinse fish and shrimp; pat dry. Cut the fish into 1-inch pieces. Cover and chill fish pieces and shrimp until needed.

2 In a large saucepan, heat olive oil over medium-high heat. Cook and stir onion, carrot, sweet pepper, and garlic in hot oil until tender. Stir in the undrained tomatoes, tomato sauce, chicken broth, wine or chicken broth, bay leaves, dried thyme (if using), Cajun seasoning, cumin, and, if desired, crushed red pepper. Bring the mixture to boiling; reduce heat. Simmer, covered, for 20 minutes.

3 Gently stir in the fish pieces, shrimp, and fresh thyme (if using). Cover and simmer for about 5 minutes more or until the fish flakes easily when tested with a fork and shrimp are opaque. Remove the bay leaves before serving.

Nutrition facts per serving: 199 cal., 5 g total fat (1 g sat. fat), 84 mg chol., 341 mg sodium, 15 g carbo., 3 g fiber, 22 g pro.

chunky CHIPOTLE PORK CHILI

For an extra burst of tongue-tingling flavor, use the 2 tablespoons chipotle chile peppers.

Start to Finish: 30 minutes
Makes: 4 servings

1 tablespoon cooking oil

1 small onion, chopped

2 teaspoons bottled minced garlic

12 ounces pork tenderloin, cut into ¾-inch cubes

2 teaspoons chili powder

2 teaspoons ground cumin

1 yellow or red sweet pepper, cut into ½-inch pieces

1 cup beer or beef broth

½ cup bottled picante sauce or salsa

1 to 2 tablespoons finely chopped canned chipotle chile peppers in adobo sauce (see tip, page 23)

1 15-ounce can small red beans or pinto beans, rinsed and drained

½ cup dairy sour cream

Fresh cilantro or parsley sprigs (optional)

1 In a large saucepan, heat oil over medium-high heat. Add onion and garlic; cook for about 3 minutes or until tender.

2 In a medium bowl, toss pork with chili powder and cumin; add to saucepan. Cook and stir until pork is browned. Add sweet pepper, beer or beef broth, picante sauce or salsa, and chipotle chile peppers. Bring to boiling; reduce heat. Cover and simmer for about 5 minutes or until pork is tender. Stir in beans; heat through. Top individual servings with sour cream. If desired, garnish with cilantro or parsley.

Nutrition facts per serving: 328 cal., 11 g total fat (4 g sat. fat), 65 mg chol., 625 mg sodium, 29 g carbo., 7 g fiber, 26 g pro.

squash AND LENTIL SOUP

The magic of this soup is garam masala, found in the spice aisle of most supermarkets. This blend of ground spices can include cinnamon, nutmeg, cloves, coriander, cumin, cardamom, pepper, chiles, fennel, and mace.

Prep: 25 minutes
Cook: 8 to 9 hours (low) or
    4 to 4½ hours (high)
Makes: 5 to 6 servings

- 1 **cup dry lentils**
- 2½ **cups peeled butternut squash, cut into ¾-inch pieces**
- ½ **cup chopped onion**
- ½ **cup chopped carrot**
- ½ **cup chopped celery**
- 2 **cloves garlic, minced**
- 1 **teaspoon garam masala**
- 4 **cups chicken broth or vegetable broth**

1 Rinse and drain lentils. In a 3½- or 4-quart slow cooker, combine lentils, squash, onion, carrot, and celery. Sprinkle garlic and garam masala over vegetables. Pour broth over all.

2 Cover and cook on low-heat setting for 8 to 9 hours or on high-heat setting for 4 to 4½ hours. Ladle into bowls.

Nutrition facts per serving: 199 cal., 2 g total fat (0 g sat. fat), 0 mg chol., 639 mg sodium, 31 g carbo., 13 g fiber, 16 g pro.

caribbean STEW WITH LIME GREMOLATA

Prep: 25 minutes
Cook: 50 minutes
Makes: 6 servings

Nonstick cooking spray

1 **pound lean boneless pork, cut into ½-inch cubes**

3 **medium onions, cut into wedges**

1 **14-ounce can reduced-sodium chicken broth**

1 **14.5-ounce can no-salt-added diced tomatoes, undrained**

1 **8-ounce can no-salt-added tomato sauce**

¼ **teaspoon cayenne pepper**

2 **medium sweet potatoes, peeled, halved lengthwise, and cut into ½-inch slices**

2 **small green, yellow, and/or red sweet peppers, seeded and cut into bite-size strips**

1 **cup canned black beans, rinsed and drained**

3 **tablespoons lime juice**

Lime Gremolata*

Lime slices and/or wedges (optional)

1 Coat an unheated 4-quart Dutch oven with nonstick cooking spray. Preheat over medium heat. Add pork to hot Dutch oven; cook and stir until brown. Add onions, chicken broth, undrained tomatoes, tomato sauce, and cayenne pepper. Bring to boiling; reduce heat. Simmer, covered, for 30 minutes.

2 Add sweet potatoes, sweet peppers, and black beans. Return to boiling; reduce heat. Simmer, covered, for about 20 minutes more or until vegetables are tender. Stir in lime juice. Top each serving with Lime Gremolata. If desired, garnish with lime slices and/or wedges.

***Lime Gremolata:** In a small bowl, stir together ½ cup snipped fresh parsley, 1 teaspoon finely shredded lime peel, and 1 clove garlic, minced.

Nutrition facts per serving: 231 cal., 4 g total fat (1 g sat. fat), 47 mg chol., 433 mg sodium, 29 g carbo., 7 g fiber, 22 g pro.

indian VEGETABLE SOUP

Chock-full of nutty garbanzo beans, red-skin potatoes, and chunks of eggplant, this curried soup makes a hearty meal.

Prep: 30 minutes
Cook: 8 to 10 hours (low) or 4 to 5 hours (high)
Makes: 6 to 8 servings

1 medium eggplant, cut into ½-inch cubes (5 to 6 cups)

1 pound red potatoes, cut into 1-inch pieces (3 cups)

2 cups chopped tomatoes or one 14.5-ounce can low-sodium tomatoes, undrained and cut up

1 15-ounce can garbanzo beans (chickpeas), rinsed and drained

1 tablespoon grated fresh ginger

1½ teaspoons mustard seeds

1½ teaspoons ground coriander

1 teaspoon curry powder

¼ teaspoon ground black pepper

4 cups vegetable broth or chicken broth

2 tablespoons snipped fresh cilantro

1 In a 4- to 6-quart slow cooker, combine eggplant, potatoes, undrained tomatoes, and garbanzo beans. Sprinkle vegetables with ginger, mustard seeds, coriander, curry powder, and pepper. Pour broth over all.

2 Cover and cook on low-heat setting for 8 to 10 hours or on high-heat setting for 4 to 5 hours. Ladle into bowls and sprinkle with cilantro.

Nutrition facts per serving: 162 cal., 2 g total fat (0 g sat. fat), 0 mg chol., 889 mg sodium, 30 g carbo., 7 g fiber, 8 g pro.

mulligatawny SOUP

Nourishing *and* delicious *are the best words to describe this hearty chicken soup. To reap all the rewards of this Indian-inspired dish, sop up the rich, curried broth with chunks of warm bread.*

Prep: 25 minutes
Cook: 35 minutes
Makes: 6 (1⅔-cup) servings

- 1 tablespoon cooking oil
- 1 cup chopped onion
- 1 cup coarsely chopped carrots
- 1 cup sliced celery
- 1⅓ cups chopped, peeled, tart apples
- 2 to 3 teaspoons curry powder
- ¼ teaspoon salt
- 3 cups reduced-sodium chicken broth
- 3 cups water
- 1 14.5-ounce can low-sodium stewed tomatoes, undrained
- 2 cups chopped cooked chicken or turkey

1 In a Dutch oven, heat cooking oil over medium heat. Cook and stir onion, carrots, and celery in hot oil for about 10 minutes or until crisp-tender. Reduce heat to medium-low; add apples, curry powder, and salt. Cook, covered, for 5 minutes. Stir in the chicken broth, water, and undrained tomatoes. Bring to boiling; reduce heat. Simmer, covered, for 10 minutes. Stir in the chicken or turkey; simmer for 10 minutes more.

Nutrition facts per serving: 197 cal., 7 g total fat (1 g sat. fat), 45 mg chol., 517 mg sodium, 17 g carbo., 4 g fiber, 17 g pro.

cajun BEAN SOUP

True Cajun cooks will tell you that it isn't the spices that make a dish authentic, it's the trio of onion, sweet peppers, and celery. The hot sauce in this recipe is optional, but it adds a spirited touch.

Start to Finish: 35 minutes
Makes: 8 (1½-cup) servings

- 2 **teaspoons cooking oil**
- 1¼ **cups chopped onion**
- 1¼ **cups chopped green sweet pepper**
- ¾ **cup finely chopped celery**
- 3 **cloves garlic, minced**
- 2½ **cups reduced-sodium chicken broth**
- 2½ **cups water**
- 1 **14.5-ounce can low-sodium stewed tomatoes, undrained**
- 2 **cups sliced fresh or frozen okra**
- 1 **15-ounce can reduced-sodium navy beans, rinsed and drained**
- 1 **15-ounce can reduced-sodium red kidney beans, rinsed and drained**
- 4 **ounces cooked smoked turkey sausage, halved lengthwise and sliced**
- 1 **bay leaf**
- 1 **teaspoon dried thyme, crushed**
- ¼ **teaspoon ground black pepper**
- ⅛ **teaspoon salt**
  Bottled hot pepper sauce (optional)
- 4 **cups hot cooked rice**

1 In a Dutch oven, heat oil over medium-high heat. Cook and stir the onion, sweet pepper, celery, and garlic in the hot oil for 8 to 10 minutes or until vegetables are tender, stirring occasionally.

2 Stir in the broth, water, undrained tomatoes, okra, beans, sausage, bay leaf, thyme, black pepper, salt, and, if desired, hot pepper sauce. Bring to boiling; reduce heat. Simmer, covered, for about 10 minutes or until okra is tender. Discard the bay leaf. Serve over hot rice.

Nutrition facts per serving: 274 cal., 4 g total fat (0 g sat. fat), 7 mg chol., 430 mg sodium, 50 g carbo., 7 g fiber, 13 g pro.

oven-baked CASSOULET

A French cassoulet traditionally is simmered for hours. Baking this version in the oven slashes the cooking time to about 40 minutes. For a touch of freshness, top with snipped parsley just before serving.

Prep: 20 minutes
Bake: 40 minutes
Makes: 5 (1⅓-cup) servings

Nonstick cooking spray

12 ounces lean boneless pork, cut into ½-inch cubes

1 teaspoon cooking oil

1 cup chopped onion

1 cup chopped carrots

3 cloves garlic, minced

2 15-ounce cans white kidney beans (cannellini beans), rinsed and drained

4 plum tomatoes, chopped

⅔ cup reduced-sodium chicken broth

⅔ cup water

2 ounces cooked turkey kielbasa, halved lengthwise and cut into ¼-inch-thick slices

1 teaspoon dried thyme, crushed

¼ teaspoon dried rosemary, crushed

¼ teaspoon ground black pepper

2 tablespoons snipped fresh parsley

1 Preheat oven to 325°F. Spray a Dutch oven with nonstick cooking spray. Preheat over medium-high heat. Cook and stir pork in Dutch oven until pork is browned. Remove pork from pan. Reduce heat. Carefully add cooking oil to hot Dutch oven. Cook the onion, carrots, and garlic in hot oil until onion is tender.

2 Stir pork, beans, tomatoes, chicken broth, water, kielbasa, thyme, rosemary, and pepper into Dutch oven. Bake, covered, for 40 to 45 minutes or until pork and carrots are tender. To serve, sprinkle each serving with parsley.

Nutrition facts per serving: 243 cal., 7 g total fat (2 g sat. fat), 38 mg chol., 497 mg sodium, 32 g carbo., 10 g fiber, 23 g pro.

Range-top method: Prepare as directed above, except instead of baking, cover and simmer about 15 minutes or until the pork and carrots are tender.

hearty PORK STEW

Prep: 25 minutes
Bake: 50 minutes
Oven: 350°F
Makes: 6 servings

1½ **pounds lean pork stew meat, cut into 1-inch pieces**

1 **teaspoon dried sage, crushed**

1 **teaspoon dried mint, crushed**

¼ **cup butter**

8 **ounces fresh button mushrooms, halved or quartered**

2 **medium onions, chopped (1 cup)**

4 **cloves garlic, minced**

1 **14-ounce can chicken broth**

1 **bay leaf**

1 **pound coarsely chopped carrots**

3 **tablespoons all-purpose flour**

1 **tablespoon Worcestershire sauce**

Hot cooked noodles

1 Preheat oven to 350°F. Sprinkle pork with sage and mint. In a 12-inch ovenproof skillet, brown pork in 1 tablespoon of the butter over medium-high heat, turning often. Remove pork from skillet. Add mushrooms, onions, and garlic to skillet. Cook and stir until onion is tender. Stir in broth, bay leaf, and browned pork. Bring mixture to boiling. Remove from heat; cover. Place skillet in oven. Bake for 30 minutes. Stir in carrots; bake, covered, for 20 minutes more or until carrots are crisp-tender.

2 In a small saucepan, melt remaining 3 tablespoons butter over medium-low heat. Remove from heat. Stir in flour and Worcestershire sauce. Transfer skillet from oven to stove top; uncover. Stir in flour mixture. Bring pork mixture to boiling over medium heat, stirring occasionally. Reduce heat. Simmer, uncovered, for 2 minutes or until slightly thickened. Remove bay leaf. Serve stew over hot cooked noodles.

Nutrition facts per serving: 409 cal., 16 g total fat (8 g sat. fat), 118 mg chol., 504 mg sodium, 36 g carbo., 4 g fiber, 29 g pro.

beer-chili BEAN SOUP

If you don't have any turkey leftovers, look for cooked turkey breast in your supermarket's meat department.

Start to Finish: 20 minutes
Makes: 4 servings

- 1 15-ounce can hot-style chili beans with chili gravy
- 1 12-ounce can beer
- 1 11.25-ounce can condensed chili beef soup
- 1½ cups chopped cooked turkey (about 8 ounces)
- 1 cup hot water
- 1 teaspoon dried minced onion
- 1 teaspoon Worcestershire sauce
- ½ teaspoon garlic powder
  Shredded cheddar cheese
  Dairy sour cream (optional)

1 In a large saucepan, combine chili beans with chili gravy, beer, chili beef soup, chopped turkey, the water, dried minced onion, Worcestershire sauce, and garlic powder.

2 Bring to boiling; reduce heat. Simmer, uncovered, for 5 minutes. Serve with cheese and, if desired, sour cream.

Nutrition facts per serving: 353 cal., 10 g total fat (5 g sat. fat), 57 mg chol., 1,154 mg sodium, 35 g carbo., 12 g fiber, 27 g pro.

super
SUPPERS

Italian Chicken, *recipe page 90*

microwave MEAT LOAF WITH TOMATO SAUCE

Prep: 15 minutes
Cook: 26 minutes
Makes: 6 servings

1 8-ounce can pizza sauce
½ cup shredded zucchini
¼ cup rolled oats
¼ cup finely chopped onion
3 tablespoons snipped fresh parsley
2 cloves garlic, minced
1 teaspoon dried thyme, crushed
¼ teaspoon salt
¼ teaspoon ground black pepper
1 pound lean ground beef
8 ounces ground turkey

1 In large bowl, combine 2 tablespoons of the pizza sauce, the zucchini, oats, onion, 2 tablespoons of the parsley, half of the garlic, the thyme, salt, and pepper. Add beef and turkey; mix well. Shape meat mixture into a 7×4×2-inch loaf. Place in a greased 9-inch microwave-safe pie plate or 2-quart square baking dish.

2 Cover meat loaf with waxed paper. Microwave on 100% power (high) for 5 minutes, turning plate once. Tilt plate slightly; spoon off drippings. In a bowl, stir together remaining pizza sauce, remaining parsley, and remaining garlic. Pour evenly over meat loaf. Cover with waxed paper; microwave on 50% power (medium) for 21 to 24 minutes or until cooked through (165°F), turning plate twice.*

Nutrition facts per serving: 243 cal., 12 g total fat (5 g sat. fat), 66 mg chol., 380 mg sodium, 7 g carbo., 1 g fiber, 24 g pro.

*There is no need to turn the plate if your microwave has a turn table.

beef WITH MUSHROOM SAUCE

For a more elegant dinner, broil beef tenderloin instead of eye round steaks and make the sauce using ⅓ cup dry red wine and ⅓ cup water in place of the vegetable juice.

Prep: 20 minutes
Broil: 10 minutes
Makes: 4 servings

⅛ teaspoon ground black pepper

4 3-ounce beef eye round steaks, trimmed of fat

1 cup sliced fresh mushrooms

½ cup sliced green onions

2 cloves garlic, minced

2 teaspoons butter or margarine

2 teaspoons cornstarch

⅔ cup low-sodium vegetable juice

½ teaspoon instant beef bouillon granules

1 Rub pepper over meat. Place meat on the unheated rack of a broiler pan. Broil 4 to 5 inches from the heat until done as desired, turning once. Allow 10 to 12 minutes for medium rare (145°F) or 12 to 15 minutes for medium (160°F).

2 Meanwhile, in a saucepan cook mushrooms, onions, and garlic in hot butter until vegetables are tender. Stir in cornstarch. Add vegetable juice and beef bouillon granules. Cook and stir until thickened and bubbly. Cook and stir for 2 minutes more. Serve the warm sauce over meat.

Nutrition facts per serving: 170 cal., 7 g total fat (3 g sat. fat), 51 mg chol., 181 mg sodium, 5 g carbo., 1 g fiber, 20 g pro.

asian FLANK STEAK

Sweet and spicy Szechwan-style cooking promises palate-pleasing diversity for your taste buds. Preparing and marinating the steak the day before allows you to pop it under the broiler and have it on the table in short order.

Prep: 15 minutes
Marinate: 4 to 24 hours
Broil: 12 minutes
Makes: 6 servings

1 1¼-pounds beef flank steak

½ cup beef broth

⅓ cup hoisin sauce

¼ cup reduced-sodium soy sauce

¼ cup sliced green onions

3 tablespoons dry sherry or apple, orange, or pineapple juice

1 tablespoon sugar

1 teaspoon grated fresh ginger

4 cloves garlic, minced

Nonstick cooking spray

1 Trim fat from beef. Place beef in a plastic bag set in a shallow dish. For marinade, in a small bowl stir together beef broth, hoisin sauce, soy sauce, green onions, sherry or juice, sugar, ginger, and garlic. Pour over beef. Close bag. Marinate in refrigerator for 4 to 24 hours, turning bag occasionally.

2 Drain beef, discarding the marinade. Spray the unheated rack of a broiler pan with nonstick cooking spray. Place beef on the prepared rack. Broil 4 to 5 inches from the heat to desired doneness, turning once. Allow 12 to 14 minutes for medium. (Or, grill the beef on the rack of an uncovered grill directly over medium coals to desired doneness, turning once. Allow 12 to 14 minutes for medium.) To serve, thinly slice beef across the grain.

Nutrition facts per serving: 144 cal., 7 g total fat (3 g sat. fat), 44 mg chol., 113 mg sodium, 1 g carbo., 0 g fiber, 18 g pro

No Beef with Beef

Protein is a vital nutrient that our bodies need for a variety of functions, such as building tissue and keeping the immune system strong. Many people enjoy meat as the primary source of protein in their diet. Red meat is one of the best sources of iron and zinc—two minerals in short dietary supply for many people. Today's beef comes from cattle that are raised to be leaner, with some cuts—such as flank and tenderloin steak—having less fat than dark meat poultry. Beef also is closely trimmed of fat by butchers. All of this makes beef a viable participant in a healthful diet.

ginger BEEF STIR-FRY

When you crave steak but not the high fat and calories that go with it, try this stir-fry. Lean beef and crispy spring vegetables make up a full-flavored dinner you can toss together in minutes.

Start to Finish: 30 minutes
Makes: 4 servings

 8 ounces beef top round steak
 ½ cup reduced-sodium beef broth
 3 tablespoons reduced-sodium soy sauce
2½ teaspoons cornstarch
 1 teaspoon sugar
 1 teaspoon grated fresh ginger
   Nonstick cooking spray
1¼ pounds fresh asparagus spears, trimmed and cut into 2-inch pieces (3 cups), or 3 cups small broccoli florets
1½ cups sliced fresh mushrooms
 4 green onions, bias-sliced into 2-inch pieces
 1 tablespoon cooking oil
 2 cups hot cooked rice

1 If desired, partially freeze beef for easier slicing. Trim fat from beef. Thinly slice beef across the grain into bite-size strips. Set aside. For sauce, in a small bowl stir together beef broth, soy sauce, cornstarch, sugar, and ginger; set aside.

2 Lightly coat an unheated wok or large skillet with nonstick cooking spray. Heat over medium-high heat. Add asparagus, mushrooms, and green onions. Stir-fry for 3 to 4 minutes or until vegetables are crisp-tender. Remove from wok or skillet.

3 Carefully add the oil to wok or skillet. Add beef; stir-fry for 2 to 3 minutes or until brown. Push the beef from center of the wok or skillet. Stir sauce. Add sauce to center of wok or skillet. Cook and stir until thickened and bubbly.

4 Return vegetables to wok or skillet. Stir all ingredients together to coat with sauce; heat through. Serve immediately over hot cooked rice.

Nutrition facts per serving: 258 cal., 7 g total fat (2 g sat. fat), 25 mg chol., 523 mg sodium, 31 g carbo., 3 g fiber, 19 g pro.

steak RÉMOULADE SANDWICHES

Served in France as an accompaniment to cold meats, fish, and seafood, the classic mayonnaise-based sauce called rémoulade brings something new to the steak sandwich.

Prep: 15 minutes
Grill: 11 minutes
Makes: 4 servings

- ¼ **cup light mayonnaise dressing or salad dressing**
- 1½ **teaspoons finely minced cornichons or gherkins**
- 1 **teaspoon capers, drained and chopped**
- ¼ **teaspoon lemon juice**
  Ground black pepper
- 2 **8-ounce boneless beef top loin steaks, cut 1 inch thick**
- 2 **teaspoons prepared garlic spread or 2 teaspoons bottled minced garlic (4 cloves)**
- 1 **large yellow sweet pepper, cut lengthwise into 8 strips**
- 4 **kaiser or French-style rolls, split and toasted**
- 1 **cup arugula or fresh spinach leaves**

1 For rémoulade, in a small bowl combine mayonnaise dressing, cornichons, capers, lemon juice, and several pinches black pepper. Cover and refrigerate until ready to serve.

2 Pat steaks dry with a paper towel. Using your fingers, rub garlic spread over steaks. Sprinkle with additional black pepper.

3 For a charcoal grill, place steaks and sweet pepper strips on the rack of an uncovered grill directly over medium coals. Grill until meat is done as desired and sweet pepper strips are crisp-tender, turning once halfway through grilling. Allow 11 to 15 minutes for medium rare (145°F) or 14 to 18 minutes for medium (160°F). (For a gas grill, preheat grill. Reduce heat to medium. Place steaks and sweet pepper strips on grill rack over heat. Cover and grill as above.) Transfer cooked steaks and sweet pepper strips to a cutting board; cut steaks into ¼-inch slices.

4 If desired, grill rolls directly over medium heat for about 1 minute or until toasted. Spread rémoulade on cut sides of toasted rolls. Fill rolls with arugula, steak slices, and sweet pepper strips. Add roll tops.

Nutrition facts per serving: 416 cal., 15 g total fat (4 g sat. fat), 62 mg chol., 517 mg sodium, 37 g carbo., 2 g fiber, 32 g pro.

feta-stuffed BURGERS

Just a little bit of feta cheese adds a rich, tangy flavor to these stuffed burgers. Feta is sometimes referred to as pickled cheese because it is stored in a salty brine similar to pickles.

Prep: 30 minutes
Grill: 12 minutes
Chill: 4 to 24 hours
Makes: 6 servings

¼ **cup refrigerated or frozen egg product, thawed**

2 **tablespoons water**

⅓ **cup rolled oats**

¼ **teaspoon ground black pepper**

⅛ **teaspoon salt**

1 **pound lean ground beef**

2 **teaspoons Dijon-style mustard**

⅓ **cup crumbled feta cheese**

3 **English muffins, split and toasted**

Tomato-Basil Relish*

Fresh basil (optional)

1 In a bowl, stir together egg product and water. Stir in oats, pepper, and salt. Add beef; mix well. Shape mixture into twelve ¼-inch-thick patties. Spread mustard on one side of 6 patties. Top with crumbled cheese. Place remaining patties on top of cheese, pressing edges to seal.

2 For charcoal grill, place patties on the rack of an uncovered grill directly over medium coals. Grill for 12 to 14 minutes or until meat is done (160°F). (For a gas grill, preheat grill. Reduce heat to medium. Place patties on grill rack over heat. Cover and grill as above.)

3 Serve patties on toasted English muffin halves. Top with Tomato-Basil Relish. If desired, garnish with fresh basil.

***Tomato-Basil Relish:** In a small bowl, stir together 2 chopped roma tomatoes; ⅓ cup chopped seeded cucumber; 2 tablespoons thinly sliced green onion; 1 tablespoon red wine vinegar; 1 tablespoon snipped, fresh basil or 1 teaspoon dried basil, crushed; and ⅛ teaspoon ground black pepper. Cover and chill for at least 4 hours or up to 24 hours.

Nutrition facts per serving: 239 cal., 10 g total fat (4 g sat. fat), 55 mg chol., 353 mg sodium, 18 g carbo., 2 g fiber, 19 g pro.

pork DIANE

Worcestershire sauce, Dijon mustard, and a double dose of lemon—fresh lemon juice and lemon-pepper seasoning—add zest to tender pork loin chops.

Start to Finish: 30 minutes
Makes: 4 servings

1   tablespoon white wine
    Worcestershire sauce
1   tablespoon water
1   teaspoon lemon juice
1   teaspoon Dijon-style mustard
4   boneless pork top loin chops,
    cut ¾ to 1 inch thick
½   to 1 teaspoon lemon-pepper
    seasoning
2   tablespoons butter or
    margarine
1   tablespoon snipped fresh
    chives or parsley

1 For sauce, in a small bowl stir together Worcestershire sauce, water, lemon juice, and mustard. Set sauce aside.

2 Sprinkle both sides of chops with lemon-pepper seasoning. In a large skillet, cook chops in hot butter over medium heat for 8 to 12 minutes or until meat is done (160°F) and juices run clear, turning once. Remove skillet from heat. Transfer chops to a serving platter; keep warm.

3 Pour sauce into skillet. Cook and stir to loosen any browned bits in bottom of skillet. Spoon sauce over chops. Sprinkle with chives.

Nutrition facts per serving: 178 cal., 11 g total fat (5 g sat. fat), 66 mg chol., 302 mg sodium, 1 g carbo., 0 g fiber, 18 g pro.

peppered PORK AND PILAF

This tantalizing pork-and-rice combo gets a quick start from vegetables culled at the salad bar.

Prep: 15 minutes
Cook: 17 minutes
Stand: 5 minutes
Makes: 4 servings

4   **boneless pork loin chops, cut ¾ inch thick**

1   **tablespoon herb-pepper seasoning**

2   **tablespoons olive oil**

2   **cups cut-up salad bar vegetables (such as sweet peppers, carrots, mushrooms, onion, and/or broccoli)**

1   **14-ounce can chicken broth**

2   **cups quick-cooking brown rice**

¼   **cup chopped roasted red sweet pepper**

1 Sprinkle both sides of meat with 2 teaspoons of the herb-pepper seasoning. In a large skillet, cook chops in 1 tablespoon of the olive oil for 5 minutes. Turn chops. Cook for 5 to 7 minutes more or until meat is done (160°F) and juices run clear.

2 Meanwhile, if necessary, cut vegetables into bite-size pieces. In a medium saucepan, heat the remaining 1 tablespoon olive oil. Add the vegetables and cook for 2 minutes. Carefully add broth. Bring to boiling. Stir in the rice, roasted pepper, and the remaining 1 teaspoon herb-pepper seasoning. Return to boiling; cover and simmer for 5 minutes. Remove from heat. Let stand for 5 minutes. Serve chops with the rice mixture.

Nutrition facts per serving: 431 cal., 20 g total fat (5 g sat. fat), 77 mg chol., 408 mg sodium, 34 g carbo., 5 g fiber, 31 g pro.

pork WITH PEACHY SALSA

Sliding the pork tenderloin slices onto skewers makes them easier to turn.

Prep: 30 minutes
Grill: 20 minutes
Makes: 6 servings

½ **cup chopped, peeled peaches
   or unpeeled nectarines**

½ **cup chopped, seeded
   cucumber**

⅓ **cup salsa**

1 **tablespoon snipped fresh
   cilantro or parsley**

12 **slices bacon**

1½ **pounds pork tenderloin
   (2 tenderloins)**

1 For salsa, in a medium bowl combine peaches, cucumber, salsa, and cilantro. Toss gently. Cover and chill for up to 2 days or until serving time.

2 In a large skillet over medium heat, partially cook bacon. Bias-cut pork tenderloin into 1½-inch slices. Wrap a slice of bacon around each piece of pork. If desired, fasten bacon to meat with wooden toothpicks. Thread wrapped meat onto skewers.

3 For a charcoal grill, in a grill with a cover arrange medium-hot coals around a drip pan. Test for medium heat above pan. Place kabobs on grill rack directly over drip pan. Cover and grill for 20 to 22 minutes or until meat juices run clear (160°F), turning once. (For a gas grill, preheat grill. Reduce heat to medium. Place kabobs on grill rack over heat. Cover and grill as above.)

4 Remove meat from skewers. Serve with salsa.

Nutrition facts per serving: 235 cal., 11 g total fat (4 g sat. fat), 87 mg chol., 338 mg sodium, 2 g carbo., 0 g fiber, 29 g pro.

grilled TURKEY MOLE

Mole (MOH-lay), a Mexican specialty, is a rich, reddish-brown sauce that contains an unexpected ingredient—chocolate. Chili powder, garlic, and tomatoes also flavor this sauce, a common accompaniment to poultry.

Prep: 25 minutes
Marinate: 2 to 4 hours
Grill: 8 minutes
Makes: 6 servings

6   **4-ounce turkey breast tenderloin steaks**

¼   **cup lime juice**

1   **tablespoon chili powder**

2   **teaspoons bottled hot pepper sauce**

1   **tablespoon margarine or butter**

½   **cup chopped onion**

2   **teaspoons sugar**

1   **clove garlic, minced**

1   **7½-ounce can tomatoes, undrained and cut up**

¼   **cup canned diced green chile peppers**

1½   **teaspoons unsweetened cocoa powder**

1½   **teaspoons chili powder**

⅛   **teaspoon salt**

    Fat-free dairy sour cream (optional)

1 Rinse turkey; pat dry. Place the turkey in a plastic bag set in a shallow dish. For marinade, in a small bowl stir together the lime juice, the 1 tablespoon chili powder, and the hot pepper sauce. Pour over turkey. Close bag. Marinate in the refrigerator for 2 to 4 hours, turning bag occasionally.

2 Meanwhile, for the mole sauce, in a medium saucepan heat margarine or butter over medium-high heat until melted. Cook and stir the onion, sugar, and garlic in hot margarine or butter for about 7 minutes or until onion is tender. Stir in the undrained tomatoes, chile peppers, cocoa powder, the 1½ teaspoons chili powder, and the salt. Bring to boiling; reduce heat. Simmer, covered, for 10 minutes. Remove from heat; set aside.

3 Drain the turkey, discarding the marinade. Grill turkey on the lightly greased rack of an uncovered grill directly over medium coals for 8 to 10 minutes or until turkey is tender and no longer pink, turning once. Serve with mole sauce and, if desired, sour cream.

Nutrition facts per serving: 156 cal., 5 g total fat (1 g sat. fat), 50 mg chol., 213 mg sodium, 6 g carbo., 1 g fiber, 22 g pro.

Turkey Talk

Turkey white meat is naturally low in fat. It has a slightly heartier taste than chicken and is versatile enough to be used as a substitute in place of higher-fat meats. Like all meats, turkey is a good source of vital iron, zinc, and vitamin B-12. If you only think of turkey at Thanksgiving, think again— whether you broil it, bake it, or grill it, turkey is a versatile meat for any time of year.

turkey PAPRIKASH

Paprikash (PAH-pree-kash) is the quintessential comfort food of Hungary. It usually is stewed with bacon drippings. We've updated the traditional method to lower the fat—but kept the rich flavor.

Prep: 25 minutes
Cook: 16 minutes
Makes: 4 servings

12 ounces turkey breast tenderloins

Nonstick cooking spray

2 teaspoons cooking oil

2 cups sliced fresh mushrooms

1 medium green sweet pepper, cut into thin, bite-size strips

1 medium onion, cut into thin wedges

2 cloves garlic, minced

2 tablespoons low-sodium tomato paste

1 tablespoon paprika

½ teaspoon dried marjoram, crushed

¼ teaspoon salt

¼ teaspoon black pepper

1 cup reduced-sodium chicken broth

1 8-ounce carton fat-free dairy sour cream

2 tablespoons all-purpose flour

2 cups hot cooked noodles

1 tablespoon snipped fresh parsley

1 Rinse turkey; pat dry. Cut the turkey crosswise into ½-inch slices. Spray a large nonstick skillet with nonstick cooking spray. Preheat skillet over medium-high heat. Brown turkey slices on both sides in skillet. Remove turkey from skillet.

2 Carefully add the oil to hot skillet; add the mushrooms, sweet pepper, onion, and garlic to skillet. Cook and stir the vegetables until crisp-tender. In a bowl, combine tomato paste, paprika, marjoram, salt, and black pepper. Gradually stir in about ½ cup of the chicken broth; add mixture to skillet. Add turkey to skillet. Bring to boiling; reduce heat. Simmer, covered, for about 15 minutes or until turkey is tender.

3 Meanwhile, stir together sour cream and flour. Stir in remaining chicken broth; add to skillet. Cook and stir until thickened and bubbly. Cook and stir for 1 minute more.

4 To serve, spoon the turkey and sauce mixture over the cooked noodles and sprinkle with parsley.

Nutrition facts per serving: 319 cal., 5 g total fat (1 g sat. fat), 37 mg chol., 386 mg sodium, 40 g carbo., 3 g fiber, 27 g pro.

chicken AND LEMON-BROCCOLI ALFREDO

Start to Finish: 20 minutes
Makes: 4 servings

4 small skinless, boneless chicken breast halves

Salt

Ground black pepper

8 ounces mushrooms, halved

1 tablespoon olive oil or cooking oil

1 lemon

3 cups broccoli florets

1 10-ounce container refrigerated light Alfredo pasta sauce

⅛ teaspoon ground black pepper

1 Season chicken with salt and pepper. In a large skillet, cook chicken and mushrooms in hot oil over medium heat for 4 minutes, turning chicken once.

2 Meanwhile, shred 2 teaspoons lemon peel; set aside. Slice lemon. Add broccoli and lemon slices to skillet. Cook, covered, for 8 minutes or until chicken is no longer pink (170°F). Place chicken and vegetables on four plates. Add Alfredo sauce, lemon peel, and ⅛ teaspoon pepper to skillet; heat through. Serve sauce with chicken.

Nutrition facts per serving: 231 cal., 11 g total fat (4 g sat. fat), 20 mg chol., 496 mg sodium, 25 g carbo., 12 g pro.

chicken WITH WHITE BEANS

White kidney beans, also called cannellini beans, are popular in the Tuscany region of Italy. As American chefs become increasingly interested in Tuscan cooking, the beans are becoming much loved stateside too.

Start to Finish: 35 minutes
Makes: 6 servings

6 skinless, boneless chicken thighs (1 pound)

1 tablespoon olive oil or cooking oil

½ cup dry white wine or water

1 teaspoon instant chicken bouillon granules

2 cloves garlic, minced

1 teaspoon dried oregano, crushed

¾ teaspoon dried thyme, crushed

½ teaspoon dried savory, crushed

⅛ teaspoon ground black pepper

1 pound banana, buttercup, or butternut squash, peeled, seeded, and cut into ½-inch pieces (about 2½ cups)

1 15-ounce can white kidney (cannellini) beans, rinsed and drained

1 14.5-ounce can diced tomatoes, undrained

2 tablespoons snipped fresh parsley

   Fresh parsley sprigs (optional)

1 In a large skillet, cook chicken in hot oil over medium-high heat until light brown, turning to brown evenly. Remove chicken from skillet. Drain off fat.

2 Add wine, bouillon granules, and garlic to skillet. Bring to boiling; reduce heat. Boil gently, uncovered, for 3 minutes or until liquid is reduced by about half, scraping up any crusty browned bits from bottom of skillet.

3 Stir in oregano, thyme, savory, and pepper. Return chicken to skillet. Add squash. Bring to boiling; reduce heat. Cover and simmer for 15 to 20 minutes or until chicken is no longer pink (180°F) and squash is nearly tender. Stir in beans and undrained tomatoes. Simmer, uncovered, for about 5 minutes more or until bean mixture is slightly thickened.

4 To serve, spoon the bean mixture into shallow bowls. Place chicken on top of bean mixture. Sprinkle with parsley. If desired, garnish with fresh parsley sprig.

Nutrition facts per serving: 219 cal., 6 g total fat (1 g sat. fat), 60 mg chol., 462 mg sodium, 21 g carbo., 5 g fiber, 21 g pro.

italian CHICKEN

This dish contains all the best ingredients Italy has to offer—black olives, capers, garlic, basil, wine, olive oil, and tomatoes. Served with a salad and warm crusty bread, it's a memorable taste of Italy from your own kitchen.

Start to Finish: 40 minutes
Makes: 4 servings

4   skinless, boneless chicken breast halves (about 1 pound)
2   tablespoons olive oil
1   large onion, halved and thinly sliced
2   cloves garlic, minced
3   large tomatoes, coarsely chopped
¼   cup Greek black olives or ripe olives, pitted and sliced
1   tablespoon capers, drained
¼   teaspoon salt
⅛   teaspoon ground black pepper
¼   cup dry red wine or reduced-sodium chicken broth
2   teaspoons cornstarch
¼   cup snipped fresh basil
2   cups hot cooked couscous

1 Rinse chicken; pat dry. In a large skillet, heat 1 tablespoon of the olive oil over medium-high heat. Add chicken; cook for 4 to 5 minutes on each side or until chicken is tender and no longer pink. Remove from pan and keep warm.

2 For sauce, add the remaining olive oil, onion, and garlic to hot skillet. Cook and stir for 2 minutes. Add the tomatoes, olives, capers, salt, and pepper to skillet. Bring to boiling; reduce heat. Simmer, covered, for 3 minutes. Stir together the wine or broth and cornstarch; add to the skillet. Cook and stir until thickened and bubbly. Cook and stir for 2 minutes more. Stir in basil. Pour sauce over chicken. Serve with couscous.

Nutrition facts per serving: 319 cal., 8 g total fat (2 g sat. fat), 59 mg chol., 289 mg sodium, 32 g carbo., 7 g fiber, 27 g pro.

asian CHICKEN AND VEGGIES

Five-spice powder, a blend available on the grocery shelf, and a bottled cooking sauce give budget chicken pieces an Asian flair.

Prep: 10 minutes
Bake: 40 minutes
Oven: 400°F
Makes: 4 servings

8   chicken drumsticks and/or thighs, skinned (2 pounds)

1   tablespoon cooking oil

1½ teaspoons five-spice powder

⅓   cup bottled plum sauce or sweet-and-sour sauce

1   14-ounce package frozen loose-pack baby whole potatoes, broccoli, carrots, baby corn, and red sweet pepper mix or one 16-ounce package frozen stir-fry vegetables (any combination)

1 Arrange chicken pieces in a 13x9x2-inch baking pan, making sure pieces don't touch. Brush chicken pieces with cooking oil; sprinkle with 1 teaspoon of the five-spice powder. Bake, uncovered, in a 400°F oven for 25 minutes.

2 Meanwhile, in a large bowl combine remaining ½ teaspoon five-spice powder and plum sauce. Add frozen vegetables; toss to coat.

3 Move chicken pieces to one side of the baking pan. Add vegetable mixture to the other side of the pan. Bake for 15 to 20 minutes more or until chicken is no longer pink (180°F), stirring vegetables once during baking. Using a slotted spoon, transfer chicken and vegetables to a serving platter.

Nutrition facts per serving: 277 cal., 9 g total fat (2 g sat. fat), 98 mg chol., 124 mg sodium, 21 g carbo., 2 g fiber, 30 g pro.

chicken-broccoli STIR-FRY

Thirty minutes to a fresh, hot, homemade stir-fry—that beats takeout any day. Seasoned with hoisin sauce and sesame oil, this stir-fry isn't missing a thing.

Start to Finish: 30 minutes
Makes: 4 servings

½ cup water

2 tablespoons soy sauce

2 tablespoons hoisin sauce

2 teaspoons cornstarch

1 teaspoon grated fresh ginger

1 teaspoon toasted sesame oil

1 pound broccoli

1 yellow sweet pepper

2 tablespoons cooking oil

12 ounces skinless, boneless chicken breasts or thighs, cut into bite-size pieces

2 cups chow mein noodles or hot cooked rice

❶ For sauce, in a small bowl stir together the water, soy sauce, hoisin sauce, cornstarch, ginger, and sesame oil. Set aside.

❷ Cut florets from broccoli stems and separate florets into small pieces. Cut broccoli stems crosswise into ¼-inch slices. Cut pepper into short, thin strips.

❸ In a wok or large skillet, heat 1 tablespoon of the cooking oil over medium-high heat. Cook and stir broccoli stems in hot oil for 1 minute. Add broccoli florets and sweet pepper; cook and stir for 3 to 4 minutes or until crisp-tender. Remove from wok; set aside.

❹ Add remaining oil to wok or skillet. Add chicken; cook and stir for 2 to 3 minutes or until no longer pink. Push chicken from center of wok. Stir sauce; pour into center of wok. Cook and stir until thickened and bubbly. Return cooked vegetables to wok; stir to coat with sauce. Cook and stir for 1 minute more or until heated through. Serve with chow mein noodles.

Nutrition facts per serving: 378 cal., 16 g total fat (3 g sat. fat), 49 mg chol., 877 mg sodium, 31 g carbo., 6 g fiber, 29 g pro.

garlic-clove CHICKEN

Cooking garlic within the clove's casing imparts only a mild garlic flavor to foods cooked with it. That's why you'll never believe 25 cloves are used here.

Prep: 20 minutes
Bake: 45 minutes
Oven: 325°F
Makes: 4 servings

Nonstick cooking spray

2 **to 2½ pounds meaty chicken pieces (breasts, thighs, and drumsticks), skinned**

25 **cloves garlic (about ½ cup or 2 to 3 bulbs)**

¼ **cup dry white wine**

Salt

Cayenne pepper

1 Preheat oven to 325°F. Lightly coat a large skillet with nonstick cooking spray. Heat skillet over medium heat. Add chicken and cook for 10 minutes, turning to brown evenly. Place chicken in a 2-quart square baking dish. Add unpeeled garlic cloves. Pour wine over chicken. Lightly sprinkle chicken with salt and cayenne pepper.

2 Bake, covered, for 45 to 50 minutes or until chicken is no longer pink (170°F for breasts, 180°F for thighs and drumsticks).

Nutrition facts per serving: 194 cal., 3 g total fat (1 g sat. fat), 96 mg chol., 232 mg sodium, 6 g carbo., 0 g fiber, 31 g pro.

roast TARRAGON CHICKEN

Tarragon's bold, aniselike flavor complements the sweetness of the roasted tomatoes and onions. You can also use rosemary or thyme.

Prep: 15 minutes
Roast: 45 minutes
Oven: 375°F
Makes: 6 servings

- 3 **tablespoons olive oil**
- 2½ **teaspoons dried tarragon, crushed**
- 2 **cloves garlic, minced**
- ½ **teaspoon coarsely ground black pepper**
- ¼ **teaspoon salt**
- 1 **pound cherry tomatoes**
- 8 **small shallots**
- 2½ **to 3 pounds meaty chicken pieces (breasts, thighs, and drumsticks)**

1 Preheat oven to 375°F. In a medium bowl, stir together olive oil, tarragon, garlic, pepper, and salt. Add tomatoes and shallots; toss gently to coat. Use a slotted spoon to remove tomatoes and shallots from bowl, reserving the olive oil mixture.

2 If desired, skin chicken. Place chicken in a shallow roasting pan. Brush chicken with the reserved olive oil mixture.

3 Roast chicken for 20 minutes. Add shallots; roast for 15 minutes. Add tomatoes; roast for 10 to 12 minutes more or until chicken is no longer pink (170°F for breasts; 180°F for thighs and drumsticks) and vegetables are tender.

Nutrition facts per serving: 266 cal., 17 g total fat (4 g sat. fat), 66 mg chol., 166 mg sodium, 6 g carbo., 1 g fiber, 21 g pro.

Roasting Vegetables

Finding ways to enhance foods' natural flavor in lieu of adding fat, salt, and sugar makes healthy eating easy. Roasting vegetables is only one of the ways to do this. Roasting (cooking with a high, dry heat) brings out the natural sugars in vegetables and concentrates their flavors. The natural flavor of the vegetables is good, but you can add any combination of dried herbs for variety.

moroccan CHICKEN

The mystique of North Africa is captured in richly flavored recipes such as this one, which are abundant in fruits and aromatic spices. Serve this rich, slow-grilled chicken dish over fluffy couscous or saffron rice.

Prep: 20 minutes
Marinate: 4 to 24 hours
Grill: 50 minutes
Makes: 4 servings

- 2 **pounds meaty chicken pieces (breasts, thighs, and drumsticks), skinned**
- ½ **cup orange juice**
- 1 **tablespoon olive oil**
- 1 **tablespoon grated fresh ginger**
- 1 **teaspoon paprika**
- 1 **teaspoon ground cumin**
- ½ **teaspoon ground coriander**
- ¼ **teaspoon crushed red pepper**
- ⅛ **teaspoon salt**
- 2 **teaspoons finely shredded orange peel**
- 2 **tablespoons honey**
- 2 **teaspoons orange juice**

1 Rinse chicken; pat dry. Place chicken in a plastic bag set in a deep dish. For the marinade, in a small bowl stir together the ½ cup orange juice, the olive oil, ginger, paprika, cumin, coriander, red pepper, and salt. Pour marinade over chicken. Close the bag. Marinate the chicken in the refrigerator for 4 to 24 hours, turning the bag occasionally.

2 Meanwhile, in a small bowl stir together the orange peel, honey, and the 2 teaspoons orange juice.

3 Drain the chicken, discarding the marinade. In a grill with a cover, arrange preheated coals around a drip pan. Test for medium heat above pan. Place chicken, skinned side up, on lightly greased grill rack over drip pan.

4 Cover and grill for 50 to 60 minutes or until the chicken is tender and no longer pink. Occasionally brush chicken with honey mixture during the last 10 minutes of grilling. (Or, to bake, place chicken, skinned side up, in a shallow baking dish. Bake, uncovered, in a 375°F oven for 45 to 55 minutes or until chicken is tender and no longer pink. Occasionally brush the chicken with the honey mixture during the last 10 minutes of baking.)

Nutrition facts per serving: 237 cal., 8 g total fat (2 g sat. fat), 92 mg chol., 98 mg sodium, 10 g carbo., 0 g fiber, 30 g pro.

sesame CHICKEN

There's no reason to think of fried chicken as permanently off-limits. For our sesame "fried" chicken recipe, we traded the frying pan for the oven and ended up with a crispy, juicy chicken that only tastes taboo.

Prep: 15 minutes
Bake: 45 minutes
Makes: 4 servings

Nonstick cooking spray

  3 **tablespoons sesame seeds**

  3 **tablespoons all-purpose flour**

  ¼ **teaspoon salt**

  ¼ **teaspoon ground red pepper**

  4 **skinless chicken breast halves (about 2 pounds)**

  3 **tablespoons reduced-sodium teriyaki sauce**

  1 **tablespoon margarine or butter, melted**

1 Preheat oven to 400°F. Spray a large baking sheet with nonstick cooking spray; set aside. In a large plastic bag, combine sesame seeds, flour, salt, and red pepper. Rinse the chicken; pat dry. Dip chicken in teriyaki sauce. Add chicken to the mixture in the plastic bag; close bag. Shake bag to coat chicken.

2 Place chicken, bone side down, on prepared baking sheet. Drizzle melted margarine or butter over chicken.

3 Bake for about 45 minutes or until chicken is tender and no longer pink.

Nutrition facts per serving: 275 cal., 11 g total fat (2 g sat. fat), 89 mg chol., 490 mg sodium, 7 g carbo., 1 g fiber, 35 g pro.

herb-pecan-crusted SNAPPER

Butter, chopped pecans, fresh herbs, and a touch of lemon and garlic make a toasty crust for meaty red snapper. This combination is terrific on fresh walleye too.

Prep: 15 minutes
Grill: 4 to 6 minutes per
    ½-inch thickness
Makes: 4 servings

4   **5- or 6-ounce fresh or frozen red snapper fillets with skin, ½ to 1 inch thick**

⅓   **cup finely chopped pecans**

2   **tablespoons fine dry bread crumbs**

2   **tablespoons butter or margarine, softened**

1   **teaspoon finely shredded lemon peel**

1   **teaspoon bottled minced garlic (2 cloves)**

1   **tablespoon snipped fresh parsley**

¼   **teaspoon salt**

⅛   **teaspoon ground black pepper**

    Pinch cayenne pepper

    Snipped fresh parsley (optional)

    Lemon wedges (optional)

① Thaw fish, if frozen; rinse and pat dry with paper towels. Measure thickness of fish. In a small bowl, combine pecans, bread crumbs, butter, lemon peel, garlic, the 1 tablespoon parsley, salt, black pepper, and cayenne pepper.

② For a charcoal grill, place fish skin side down on the greased rack of an uncovered grill directly over medium coals. Spoon pecan mixture on top of fillets; spread slightly. Grill until fish flakes easily when tested with a fork. Allow 4 to 6 minutes per ½-inch thickness of fish. (For a gas grill, preheat grill. Reduce heat to medium. Place fish on greased grill rack over heat. Spoon pecan mixture on top of fillets; spread slightly. Cover and grill as above.) If desired, sprinkle fish with additional snipped parsley and serve with lemon wedges.

Nutrition facts per serving: 276 cal., 16 g total fat (5 g sat. fat), 68 mg chol., 395 mg sodium, 4 g carbo., 1 g fiber, 31 g pro.

snapper VERACRUZ

Snapper Veracruz, one of Mexico's best-known fish recipes, is a melding of flavors. The recipe includes Spanish green olives and capers with jalapeño peppers from Jalapa, the capital of the state of Veracruz.

Start to Finish: 30 minutes
Makes: 6 servings

1½ **pounds fresh or frozen skinless red snapper or other fish fillets, ½ to ¾ inch thick**

⅛ **teaspoon salt**

⅛ **teaspoon ground black pepper**

1 **large onion, sliced and separated into rings**

2 **cloves garlic, minced**

1 **tablespoon cooking oil**

2 **large tomatoes, chopped (2 cups)**

¼ **cup sliced pimiento-stuffed green olives**

¼ **cup dry white wine**

2 **tablespoons capers, drained**

1 **to 2 fresh jalapeño or serrano chile peppers, seeded and chopped (see tip, page 23), or 1 to 2 canned jalapeño chile peppers, rinsed, drained, seeded, and chopped**

½ **teaspoon sugar**

1 **bay leaf**

❶ Thaw fish, if frozen. Rinse fish; pat dry with paper towels. Cut fish into 6 serving-size pieces. Sprinkle fish with salt and black pepper.

❷ For sauce, in a large skillet cook onion and garlic in hot oil until onion is tender. Stir in tomatoes, olives, wine, capers, jalapeño peppers, sugar, and bay leaf. Bring to boiling. Add fish to skillet. Return to boiling; reduce heat. Cover and simmer for 6 to 10 minutes or until fish flakes easily when tested with a fork. Use a slotted spatula to carefully transfer fish from skillet to a serving platter. Cover and keep warm.

❸ Gently boil sauce in skillet for 5 to 6 minutes or until reduced to about 2 cups, stirring occasionally. Discard bay leaf. Spoon sauce over fish.

Nutrition facts per serving: 178 cal., 6 g total fat (1 g sat. fat), 41 mg chol., 384 mg sodium, 6 g carbo., 1 g fiber, 25 g pro.

salmon WITH MANGO SALSA

The mango is more than just another pretty fruit. It's a nutrition powerhouse that contains generous amounts of vitamins A, C, and E plus lots of fiber.

Prep: 15 minutes
Grill: 20 minutes
Marinate: 4 hours
Makes: 4 servings

4 **6- to 8-ounce fresh or frozen salmon fillets (with skin), 1 inch thick**

2 **tablespoons sugar**

1½ **teaspoons finely shredded lime peel**

¾ **teaspoon salt**

¼ **teaspoon cayenne pepper**

1 **large ripe mango, peeled, seeded, and cut into thin, bite-size strips**

½ **of a medium cucumber, seeded and cut into thin, bite-size strips**

2 **green onions, sliced**

3 **tablespoons lime juice**

1 **tablespoon snipped fresh cilantro or 2 teaspoons snipped fresh mint**

1 **small fresh jalapeño chile pepper, seeded and chopped (see tip, page 23)**

1 **clove garlic, minced**

① Thaw fish, if frozen. Rinse fish; pat dry. Place fish skin side down in a shallow dish.

② For rub, in a small bowl stir together sugar, lime peel, ½ teaspoon of the salt, and the cayenne pepper. Sprinkle rub evenly over fish; rub in with your fingers. Cover and marinate in the refrigerator for 4 to 24 hours.

③ Meanwhile, for salsa, in a medium bowl combine mango, cucumber, green onions, lime juice, cilantro, jalapeño pepper, garlic, and remaining ¼ teaspoon salt. Cover and chill until ready to serve.

④ In a grill with a cover, arrange medium-hot coals around a drip pan. Test for medium heat above the pan. Place fish skin side down on the greased grill rack directly over drip pan, tucking under any thin edges. Cover and grill for 20 to 25 minutes or until fish flakes easily when tested with a fork. If desired, remove skin from fish. Serve fish with salsa.

Nutrition facts per serving: 352 cal., 15 g total fat (3 g sat. fat), 105 mg chol., 520 mg sodium, 18 g carbo., 2 g fiber, 37 g pro.

company's COMING

Chili-Glazed Pork Roast, *recipe page 112*

herbed BEEF TENDERLOIN

Stir fresh parsley, rosemary, and thyme into Dijon mustard to create a flavorful herb rub for roast beef. Mustard-spiked sour cream makes a refreshing condiment.

Prep: 5 minutes
Roast: 30 minutes
Stand: 15 minutes
Oven: 325°F
Makes: 8 servings

1 **2-pound beef tenderloin roast**
¼ **cup snipped fresh parsley**
2 **tablespoons Dijon-style mustard**
1 **tablespoon snipped fresh rosemary**
2 **teaspoons snipped fresh thyme**
1 **teaspoon olive oil or cooking oil**
½ **teaspoon coarsely ground black pepper**
2 **cloves garlic, minced**
½ **cup light dairy sour cream**
2 **teaspoons Dijon-style mustard**
 Coarsely ground black pepper

1 Preheat oven to 325°F. Trim fat from meat. In small bowl, stir together parsley, the 2 tablespoons mustard, the rosemary, thyme, oil, pepper, and garlic. Rub over top and sides of meat.

2 Place meat on a rack in a shallow roasting pan. Insert a meat thermometer into center of meat. Roast for 30 to 45 minutes or until meat thermometer registers 135°F. Cover with foil and let stand 15 minutes. (The meat's temperature will rise 10°F while it stands.)

3 Meanwhile, for sauce, stir together sour cream and the 2 teaspoons mustard. Thinly slice meat. Serve with sauce. If desired, sprinkle with additional pepper.

Nutrition facts per serving: 215 cal., 11 g total fat (4 g sat. fat), 75 mg chol., 178 mg sodium, 2 g carbo., 0 g fiber, 25 g pro.

wine-balsamic-glazed
STEAK

Start to Finish: 30 minutes
Makes: 4 servings

2　teaspoons cooking oil

1　pound boneless beef top loin or top sirloin steak, cut ½ to ¾ inch thick

3　cloves garlic, minced

⅛　teaspoon crushed red pepper

¾　cup dry red wine

2　cups sliced fresh mushrooms

3　tablespoons balsamic vinegar

2　tablespoons soy sauce

4　teaspoons honey

2　tablespoons butter

1 In a large skillet, heat oil over medium-high heat until very hot. Add steak. Reduce heat to medium and cook, uncovered, for 10 to 13 minutes or to desired doneness, turning meat occasionally. Allow 10 to 13 minutes for medium rare (145°F) to medium (160°F). If meat browns too quickly, reduce heat to medium low. Transfer meat to platter and keep warm.

2 Add garlic and red pepper to skillet; cook for 10 seconds. Remove skillet from heat. Carefully add wine. Return to heat. Boil, uncovered, for about 5 minutes or until most of the liquid is evaporated. Add mushrooms, vinegar, soy sauce, and honey; return to simmer. Cook and stir for about 4 minutes or until mushrooms are tender. Stir in butter until melted. Spoon over steak.

Nutrition facts per serving: 377 cal., 21 g total fat (9 g sat. fat), 82 mg chol., 588 mg sodium, 12 g carbo., 0 g fiber, 27 g pro.

honey-ancho-glazed BEEF TENDERLOIN

Soak: 1 hour
Prep: 20 minutes
Grill: 35 minutes
Stand: 15 minutes
Makes: 8 to 10 servings

- 2 **to 3 cups hickory wood chips**
- ¼ **cup honey**
- 1½ **teaspoons ground ancho chile pepper or chili powder**
- 2 **tablespoons cooking oil**
- 1 **3- to 4-pound beef tenderloin roast**
- 1 **teaspoon salt**
- 1 **teaspoon ground black pepper**

1 At least 1 hour before grilling, soak wood chips in enough water to cover. Drain before using.

2 In a small saucepan, combine honey and chile pepper. Cook and stir over medium-low heat until heated through. Remove from heat. Stir in oil. Brush some of the mixture over roast. Sprinkle roast with salt and black pepper.

3 In a grill with a cover, arrange preheated coals around a drip pan. Test for medium heat above drip pan. Sprinkle wood chips over coals. Pour 1 inch of water into drip pan. Place roast on grill rack over drip pan. Cover and grill for 35 to 45 minutes or until an instant-read thermometer inserted near the center of the roast registers 135°F, brushing with honey mixture occasionally during the first 20 minutes. Discard any remaining honey mixture.

4 Remove roast from grill. Cover; let stand for 15 minutes before slicing. (The temperature of the meat will rise 10°F during standing.)

Nutrition facts per serving: 325 cal., 17 g total fat (4 g sat. fat), 78 mg chol., 360 mg sodium, 18 g carbo., 0 g fiber, 27 g pro.

pork CHOPS WITH GORGONZOLA AND PEARS

Prep: 10 minutes
Cook: 20 minutes
Makes: 4 servings

4 **pork rib chops, cut ¾ to 1 inch thick**

Sea salt, kosher salt, or salt

2 **tablespoons olive oil**

2 **medium ripe pears, peeled, cored, and cut into 8 wedges each**

2 **tablespoons butter**

¼ **cup dry white wine or apple juice**

¼ **cup whipping cream**

8 **ounces creamy Gorgonzola or blue cheese, crumbled**

Ground black pepper

1 Sprinkle pork chops with salt. In a 12-inch skillet, cook chops in hot oil over medium heat for 5 minutes. Turn chops and cook for 5 minutes more or until brown and juices run clear (160°F). Transfer chops to a serving platter. Drain fat from skillet.

2 In same skillet, cook pear wedges in butter over medium-high heat for 5 minutes or until brown, turning once. Add pears to platter.

3 For sauce, add wine and cream to skillet. Bring to boiling; reduce heat. Boil gently, uncovered, for 1 to 2 minutes or until slightly thickened. Add Gorgonzola; whisk until cheese almost melts. Remove from heat. Serve with pork and pears. Sprinkle with pepper.

Nutrition facts per serving: 618 cal., 46 g total fat (24 g sat. fat), 147 mg chol., 1,105 mg sodium, 14 g carbo., 4 g fiber, 34 g pro.

chili-glazed PORK ROAST

Prep: 20 minutes
Roast: 1¼ hours
Stand: 15 minutes
Oven: 325°F
Makes: 8 to 10 servings

1 **tablespoon packed brown sugar**

1 **tablespoon snipped fresh thyme or 1 teaspoon dried thyme, crushed**

1 **teaspoon chili powder**

1 **teaspoon snipped fresh rosemary or ¼ teaspoon dried rosemary, crushed**

⅛ **teaspoon cayenne pepper**

1 **2- to 2½-pound boneless pork top loin roast (single loin)**

Fresh rosemary sprigs (optional)

1 Preheat oven to 325°F. In a small bowl, combine brown sugar, thyme, chili powder, rosemary, and cayenne pepper. Sprinkle mixture evenly over roast; rub in with your fingers.

2 Place roast on a rack in a shallow roasting pan. Insert a meat thermometer into center of roast. Roast for 1¼ to 1½ hours or until thermometer registers 155°F. Cover roast with foil; and let stand for 15 minutes (the temperature of the meat will rise 5°F during standing). If desired, garnish serving platter with rosemary.

Nutrition facts per serving: 134 cal., 4 g total fat (2 g sat. fat), 50 mg chol., 37 mg sodium, 2 g carbo., 0 g fiber, 20 g pro.

mustard-maple PORK ROAST

Dijon mustard and maple syrup make a wonderful glaze for pork. Let the roast stand for 15 minutes before carving—this allows the temperature to rise to 160°F and makes the roast easier to slice.

Prep: 20 minutes
Roast: 1½ hours
Stand: 15 minutes
Oven: 325°F
Makes: 8 to 10 servings

1 **2- to 2½-pound boneless pork loin roast (single loin)**

2 **tablespoons Dijon-style mustard**

1 **tablespoon maple-flavor syrup**

2 **teaspoons dried sage, crushed**

1 **teaspoon finely shredded orange peel**

¼ **teaspoon salt**

¼ **teaspoon ground black pepper**

20 **to 24 tiny new potatoes (about 1¾ pounds)**

16 **ounces packaged peeled baby carrots**

1 **tablespoon olive oil**

¼ **teaspoon salt**

1 Preheat oven to 325°F. Trim fat from meat. Stir together mustard, syrup, sage, orange peel, the ¼ teaspoon salt, and the pepper. Spoon mixture onto meat. Place roast fat side up on a rack in a shallow roasting pan. Insert a meat thermometer. Roast, uncovered, for 45 minutes.

2 Meanwhile, peel a strip of skin from the center of each potato. Cook potatoes in boiling salted water for 5 minutes. Add carrots; cook for 5 minutes more. Drain.

3 Toss together potatoes, carrots, olive oil, and ¼ teaspoon salt. Place in roasting pan around pork roast. Roast, uncovered, for 45 minutes to 1 hour more or until meat thermometer registers 155°F. Cover with foil and let stand for 15 minutes. (The meat's temperature will rise 5°F while it stands.)

Nutrition facts per serving: 281 cal., 10 g total fat (3 g sat. fat), 51 mg chol., 309 mg sodium, 29 g carbo., 3 g fiber, 19 g pro.

chicken VENETO

Start to Finish: 30 minutes
Makes: 4 servings

8   ounces dried fettuccine or linguine

12 ounces skinless, boneless chicken breast halves

2   tablespoons extra-virgin olive oil

¼   cup butter

3   cloves garlic, minced

1   9-ounce package frozen artichoke hearts, thawed and halved

¼   cup coarsely chopped pistachios

¾   cup dry white wine

¼   teaspoon salt

2   tablespoons snipped fresh parsley

Cracked black pepper

1 Cook pasta according to package directions. Drain; keep warm.

2 Meanwhile, cut chicken into bite-size strips. In a very large skillet, cook chicken in hot oil over medium-high heat for 3 to 4 minutes or until chicken is no longer pink. Remove chicken from skillet; discard pan drippings.

3 In the same skillet, melt butter over medium heat. Add garlic; cook and stir for 15 seconds. Remove from heat. Add artichokes, pistachios, and wine. Return to heat. Bring to boiling; reduce heat. Simmer, uncovered, for 5 minutes. Stir in salt. Return chicken to skillet. Cook for 1 to 2 minutes more or until heated through.

4 Spoon chicken mixture over pasta. Sprinkle with parsley and cracked black pepper. Serve immediately.

Nutrition facts per serving: 583 cal., 25 g total fat (8 g sat. fat), 82 mg chol., 325 mg sodium, 51 g carbo., 6 g fiber, 31 g pro.

pecan-crusted CHICKEN

Prep: 20 minutes
Cook: 12 minutes
Makes: 4 servings

2 tablespoons orange
   marmalade

2 tablespoons pure maple
   syrup

1 cup finely chopped pecans

3 tablespoons all-purpose flour

¼ teaspoon salt

4 skinless, boneless chicken
   breast halves

2 tablespoons cooking oil

1 tablespoon butter

1 In a small bowl, stir together orange marmalade and maple syrup; set aside. In a shallow dish, combine pecans, flour, and salt. Brush marmalade mixture on both sides of chicken breast halves. Dip into pecan mixture to coat, pressing pecan mixture into chicken, if necessary.

2 In a 12-inch skillet, heat cooking oil and butter over medium heat until mixture begins to bubble. Add chicken breasts and cook for 6 minutes. Turn chicken. Cook for 6 to 9 minutes more or until golden brown and no longer pink in center (170°F). Watch closely and reduce heat if chicken browns too quickly.

Nutrition facts per serving: 506 cal., 32 g total fat (5 g sat. fat), 90 mg chol., 279 mg sodium, 21 g carbo., 3 g fiber, 36 g pro.

chicken MEDALLIONS WITH MUSTARD SAUCE

Start to Finish: 25 minutes
Makes: 4 servings

4 **skinless, boneless chicken breast halves**

Salt and ground black pepper

2 **tablespoons olive oil or cooking oil**

¼ **cup dry white wine**

2 **tablespoons crème fraiche**

2 **tablespoons tarragon mustard or dill mustard**

1 Place each chicken breast half between two pieces of plastic wrap. With the flat side of a meat mallet, pound lightly to a ½-inch thickness. Remove plastic wrap. Sprinkle chicken with salt and pepper.

2 In a 12-inch skillet, cook chicken breasts, two at a time, in hot oil over medium-high heat for 2 to 3 minutes or until golden, turning once. Transfer chicken to a serving platter; keep warm.

3 For sauce, carefully add wine to hot skillet. Cook and stir until bubbly, loosening any brown bits in bottom of skillet. Add crème fraiche and mustard to skillet; stir with a wire whisk until combined. Spoon sauce over chicken.

Nutrition facts per serving: 255 cal., 11 g total fat (3 g sat. fat), 92 mg chol., 306 mg sodium, 1 g carbo., 0 g fiber, 33 g pro.

spicy GRILLED SHRIMP

Prep: 15 minutes
Marinate: 1 hour
Grill: 7 minutes
Makes: 4 servings

1½ **pounds fresh or frozen peeled and deveined extra-large shrimp**

¼ **cup orange marmalade**

¼ **cup honey**

2 **to 3 teaspoons Cajun seasoning**

1 **tablespoon olive oil**

1 Thaw shrimp, if frozen. If using wooden skewers, soak in water for 1 hour. Rinse shrimp; pat dry. For sauce, in a small saucepan, stir together marmalade, honey, and ½ teaspoon of the Cajun seasoning; set aside.

2 Place shrimp in a self-sealing plastic bag set in a shallow bowl. For marinade, in a small bowl combine oil and remaining Cajun seasoning. Pour marinade over shrimp. Seal bag. Marinate shrimp in refrigerator for 1 hour, turning bag occasionally.

3 Drain shrimp, discarding marinade. Thread shrimp onto skewers. For a charcoal grill, place skewers on the greased rack of an uncovered grill directly over medium coals. Grill for 7 to 9 minutes or until shrimp are opaque, turning once halfway through grilling. (For a gas grill, preheat grill. Reduce heat to medium. Place skewers on greased grill rack over heat. Cover and grill as above.)

4 Stir marmalade sauce over low heat for 2 to 3 minutes or until melted. Drizzle sauce over shrimp on skewers. Serve shrimp on skewers.

Nutrition facts per serving: 430 cal., 7 g total fat (1 g sat. fat), 259 mg chol., 357 mg sodium, 55 g carbo., 1 g fiber, 37 g pro.

cajun SHRIMP PASTA WITH ANDOUILLE CREAM SAUCE

Often used in Cajun cooking, andouille (ahn-DOO-ee) is a pork sausage seasoned with salt, pepper, and garlic and smoked over pecan wood. Outside Louisiana's Cajun country the real thing can be hard to find. Look for it at a specialty food store. Or substitute kielbasa and add a little cayenne pepper.

Start to Finish: 40 minutes
Makes: 8 servings

- 1 **pound fresh or frozen peeled and deveined large shrimp**
- 1 **pound dried bowtie pasta**
- 1 **cup chopped sweet onion (1 large)**
- 1 **tablespoon olive oil**
- 3 **to 4 teaspoons Cajun seasoning**
- 1 **10-ounce container refrigerated Alfredo pasta sauce**
- ½ **cup milk**
- 4 **ounces smoked cheddar cheese, shredded (1 cup)**
- 4 **ounces cooked andouille sausage, chopped**
- 1 **cup chopped tomatoes**
  Grated Parmesan cheese
  Sliced green onions

1 Thaw shrimp, if frozen. Set aside. Cook pasta according to package directions; drain and return to pan. Keep warm.

2 Meanwhile, in a 12-inch skillet, cook onion in hot oil over medium heat for 5 to 10 minutes or until tender, stirring occasionally. Stir in Cajun seasoning. Add shrimp. Cook for 2 to 4 minutes or until shrimp are opaque, stirring occasionally. Reduce heat to low.

3 Stir in Alfredo sauce, milk, and cheese. Cook and stir over low heat until cheese melts. Stir in sausage and tomatoes. Add shrimp mixture to hot pasta; toss gently to coat. Sprinkle with Parmesan cheese and green onions.

Nutrition facts per serving: 473 cal., 17 g total fat (8 g sat. fat), 136 mg chol., 629 mg sodium, 51 g carbo., 3 g fiber, 29 g pro.

coconut SHRIMP WITH CHUTNEY

Start to Finish: 15 minutes
Oven: 400°F
Makes: 10 servings

1 **pound fresh or frozen peeled and deveined shrimp**

1 **cup flaked coconut, toasted and chopped**

½ **cup seasoned fine dry bread crumbs**

¾ **teaspoon curry powder**

2 **egg whites, lightly beaten**

Nonstick cooking spray

½ **cup mango chutney**

¼ **cup orange juice**

¼ **teaspoon ground ginger**

1 Thaw shrimp, if frozen. Rinse shrimp; pat dry with paper towels. Preheat oven to 400°F. Generously grease a 15×10×1-inch baking pan; set aside.

2 In a shallow bowl, combine coconut, bread crumbs, and curry powder. Place egg whites in another small shallow bowl. Dip shrimp into egg whites, then into coconut mixture, pressing it firmly onto shrimp. Place in prepared baking pan. Coat shrimp with nonstick cooking spray.

3 Bake for about 10 minutes or until shrimp are opaque. Meanwhile, in a small bowl, combine chutney, orange juice, and ginger. Serve with shrimp.

Nutrition facts per serving: 138 cal., 4 g total fat (3 g sat. fat), 69 mg chol., 290 mg sodium, 14 g carbo., 1 g fiber, 11 g pro.

chipotle-sauced CRAB CAKES

This recipe is a restaurant favorite, but our version is super-simple to whip up at home. To tame the spiciness of the Chipotle Sauce, remove the seeds from the pepper before you add it to the rest of the ingredients.

Start to Finish: 30 minutes
Makes: 4 servings

- 1 **egg, slightly beaten**
- ¾ **cup soft bread crumbs (1 slice)**
- 2 **tablespoons sliced green onion**
- 2 **tablespoons mayonnaise or salad dressing**
- 1 **tablespoon milk**
- ½ **teaspoon lemon-pepper seasoning**
- 2 **6.5-ounce cans crabmeat, drained, flaked, and cartilage removed**
  Nonstick cooking spray
- 4 **cups torn mixed salad greens**
  Chipotle Sauce*

1 In a large bowl, stir together egg, bread crumbs, green onion, mayonnaise, milk, and lemon-pepper seasoning. Add crabmeat; mix well. Shape into eight 2½-inch patties.

2 Lightly coat an unheated large nonstick skillet with nonstick cooking spray. Preheat over medium heat. Add crab patties. Cook for 6 to 8 minutes or until browned, turning once. Serve crab patties with greens and Chipotle Sauce.

***Chipotle Sauce:** In a small bowl, stir together ⅓ cup mayonnaise or salad dressing; ¼ cup dairy sour cream; 2 tablespoons milk; 2 teaspoons snipped fresh cilantro; 1 canned chipotle chile pepper in adobo sauce, drained and finely chopped (see tip, page 23); and pinch salt.

Nutrition facts per serving: 359 cal., 26 g total fat (6 g sat. fat), 150 mg chol., 712 mg sodium, 8 g carbo., 1 g fiber, 23 g pro.

salmon CONFETTI CHOWDER

If watercress isn't available, use snipped fresh parsley, spinach, or basil.

Start to Finish: 25 minutes
Makes: 4 servings

- **2 cups frozen (yellow, green, and red) sweet pepper and onion stir-fry vegetables**
- **2 tablespoons minced seeded fresh jalapeño chile peppers (see tip, page 23)**
- **1 tablespoon butter or margarine**
- **2 tablespoons all-purpose flour**
- **2 cups milk**
- **1 cup half-and-half or light cream**
- **2 cups refrigerated diced potatoes with onions**
- **1 15-ounce can salmon, drained and flaked**
- **¼ cup snipped fresh watercress**
- **½ teaspoon finely shredded lemon peel**
- **½ teaspoon salt**
- **½ teaspoon ground black pepper**

1 In a large saucepan, cook stir-fry vegetables and chile peppers in hot butter for 3 to 5 minutes or until tender. Stir in flour. Stir in milk and half-and-half. Cook and stir until slightly thickened. Cook and stir for 2 minutes more.

2 Stir in diced potatoes, salmon, watercress, shredded lemon peel, salt, and black pepper. Cook and stir until chowder is heated through.

Nutrition facts per serving: 410 cal., 17 g total fat (8 g sat. fat), 40 mg chol., 531 mg sodium, 30 g carbo., 3 g fiber, 34 g pro.

citrus-glazed SALMON

To save even more time, look for bottled grated ginger in your supermarket's produce section.

Prep: 15 minutes
Bake: 4 minutes per ½-inch thickness
Oven: 450°F
Makes: 8 servings

- 1 **2-pound fresh or frozen salmon fillet, skin removed**
- **Salt**
- **Ground black pepper**
- ¾ **cup orange marmalade**
- 2 **green onions, sliced**
- 2 **teaspoons dry white wine**
- 1 **teaspoon grated fresh ginger**
- 1 **teaspoon Dijon-style mustard**
- ½ **teaspoon bottled minced garlic**
- ¼ **teaspoon cayenne pepper**
- ⅛ **teaspoon five-spice powder**
- 3 **tablespoons sliced almonds, toasted**
- **Steamed fresh asparagus spears* (optional)**

1 Thaw fish, if frozen. Preheat oven to 450°F. Rinse fish; pat dry with paper towels. Measure the thickest portion of the fish fillet. Sprinkle with salt and pepper. Place in shallow baking pan; set aside.

2 In a small bowl, stir together marmalade, green onions, wine, ginger, mustard, garlic, cayenne pepper, and five-spice powder. Spoon over fish.

3 Bake for 4 to 6 minutes per ½-inch thickness or until fish flakes easily when tested with a fork. Sprinkle individual servings with almonds. If desired, serve fish with asparagus.

Nutrition facts per serving: 227 cal., 6 g total fat (1 g sat. fat), 59 mg chol., 170 mg sodium, 21 g carbo., 1 g fiber, 24 g pro.

*Test Kitchen Tip: To steam fresh asparagus, snap off and discard woody bases from spears. Steam spears for 4 to 6 minutes or until tender.

pan-seared TILAPIA WITH ALMOND BROWNED BUTTER

Pan-searing gives the fish a golden crust and locks in flavor and natural juices. If you try to turn the fish fillets and there's some resistance, cook them a little longer, and try again.

Start to Finish: 25 minutes
Makes: 4 servings

- 4 4- to 5-ounce skinless fresh or frozen tilapia fillets or other white fish
- 3 cups fresh pea pods, trimmed
   Salt
   Ground black pepper
- 1 teaspoon all-purpose flour
- 1 tablespoon olive oil
- 2 tablespoons butter
- ¼ cup coarsely chopped almonds
- 1 tablespoon snipped fresh parsley

❶ Thaw fish, if frozen. Rinse fish; pat dry with paper towels. Set aside. In a large saucepan, bring a large amount of lightly salted water to boiling. Add pea pods; cook for 2 minutes. Drain; set aside.

❷ Meanwhile, sprinkle one side of each fish fillet with salt and pepper; sprinkle with the flour. Preheat a large skillet over medium-high heat. When skillet is hot (a drop of water should sizzle or roll), remove from heat; immediately add oil, tilting skillet to coat with oil. Return skillet to heat; add fish, floured sides up (if necessary, cook fish half at a time). Cook fish for 4 to 5 minutes or until it is easy to move with a spatula. Gently turn fish; cook for 2 to 3 minutes more or until fish flakes easily when tested with a fork. Arrange pea pods on a serving platter; arrange fish on top of pea pods.

❸ Reduce heat to medium. Add butter to the skillet. When butter begins to melt, stir in almonds. Cook for 30 to 60 seconds or until nuts are lightly toasted (do not let butter burn). Spoon butter mixture over fish. Sprinkle with parsley.

Nutrition facts per serving: 266 cal., 15 g total fat (5 g sat. fat), 71 mg chol., 210 mg sodium, 7 g carbo., 3 g fiber, 24 g pro.

broiled HALIBUT WITH DIJON CREAM

Your guests will "ooh" and "ahh" over this special dish. If there are no halibut steaks at the fish counter, feel free to try sea bass or cod instead.

Start to Finish: 15 minutes
Makes: 4 servings

- **4** fresh or frozen halibut steaks, cut 1 inch thick (1 to 1½ pounds total)
- **1** teaspoon Greek-style seasoning blend
- **¼** teaspoon coarsely ground black pepper
- **¼** cup dairy sour cream
- **¼** cup creamy Dijon-style mustard blend
- **1** tablespoon milk
- **½** teaspoon dried oregano, crushed

1 Preheat broiler. Thaw fish, if frozen. Rinse fish; pat dry with paper towels. Grease the unheated rack of a broiler pan; place fish on rack. Sprinkle fish with Greek-style seasoning blend and pepper.

2 Broil 4 inches from the heat for 8 to 12 minutes or until fish flakes easily when tested with a fork, turning once halfway through broiling. Invert fish onto a serving platter.

3 Meanwhile, for sauce: In a small bowl, combine sour cream, mustard blend, milk, and oregano. Serve sauce over fish.

Nutrition facts per serving: 168 cal., 5 g total fat (2 g sat. fat), 42 mg chol., 300 mg sodium, 4 g carbo., 0 g fiber, 24 g pro.

Pick a Blend

Herb and spice blends save you the time of measuring a number of seasonings. The Greek-style seasoning used in Broiled Halibut with Dijon Cream is typically a mix of lemon, garlic, and oregano plus other flavorings. Because each brand is different, try several until you find the one you like best. Other blends include Cajun seasoning, Italian seasoning, fines herbes, herbes de Provence, lemon-pepper seasoning, and Jamaican jerk seasoning.

one-dish
DINNERS

Salmon with Feta and Pasta, *recipe page 156*

bowties WITH MUSHROOMS AND SPINACH

This mushroom, vegetable, and pasta combo makes a savory side dish that takes almost no time. Remember this recipe next time you need a great side dish for grilled or roasted meat.

Prep: 10 minutes
Cook: 10 minutes
Makes: 4 servings

6 **ounces dried farfalle (bowties)**

1 **medium onion, chopped (½ cup)**

1 **cup sliced portobello or other fresh mushrooms**

2 **cloves garlic, minced**

1 **tablespoon olive oil**

4 **cups thinly sliced fresh spinach**

1 **teaspoon snipped fresh thyme**

⅛ **teaspoon ground black pepper**

2 **tablespoons shredded Parmesan cheese**

1 Cook farfalle according to package directions. Drain well.

2 Meanwhile, in a large skillet, cook and stir onion, mushrooms, and garlic in hot oil over medium heat for 2 to 3 minutes or until mushrooms are nearly tender. Stir in spinach, thyme, and pepper; cook for 1 minute or until heated through and spinach is slightly wilted. Stir in cooked pasta; toss gently to mix. Sprinkle with cheese.

Nutrition facts per serving: 219 cal., 5 g total fat (1 g sat. fat), 2 mg chol., 86 mg sodium, 35 g carbo., 4 g fiber, 9 g pro.

fettuccine WITH CHERRY TOMATOES

Start to Finish: 20 minutes
Makes: 4 servings

1　**9-ounce package refrigerated fettuccine, cut into thirds**

½　**cup shredded Parmesan cheese**

2　**tablespoons olive oil**

1　**6- to 9-ounce package refrigerated or frozen Italian-flavor or grilled cooked chicken breast strips, thawed if frozen**

1　**pint cherry tomatoes, halved**

½　**cup pitted ripe olives, halved**

　　Salt

　　Ground black pepper

1 In a Dutch oven, cook pasta according to package directions. Drain and return to pan.

2 Add cheese, oil, and chicken. Return to low heat; toss to coat and heat through. Remove from heat. Add tomatoes and olives. Season with salt and pepper to taste and toss again. Serve immediately.

Nutrition facts per serving: 371 cal., 15 g total fat (4 g sat. fat), 76 mg chol., 866 mg sodium, 39 g carbo., 3 g fiber, 22 g pro.

rotini BAKE

Prep: 40 minutes
Bake: 35 minutes
Stand: 10 minutes
Oven: 375°F
Makes: 8 servings

12 ounces dried rotini

½ cup bottled balsamic
vinaigrette

1 15-ounce can white kidney
(cannellini) or garbanzo
beans, rinsed and drained

8 ounces feta cheese, crumbled

1 cup coarsely chopped pitted
Greek black olives

1 pound roma tomatoes,
coarsely chopped

½ cup seasoned fine dry bread
crumbs

1 8-ounce carton low-fat plain
yogurt

¾ cup milk

⅓ cup grated Parmesan cheese

1 tablespoon all-purpose flour

1 Preheat oven to 375°F. Lightly grease a 3-quart rectangular baking dish; set aside. Cook pasta according to package directions. Drain. In a very large bowl, combine vinaigrette and pasta; toss to coat. Stir in beans, cheese, olives, and tomatoes.

2 Sprinkle ¼ cup of the bread crumbs into prepared dish. Spoon pasta mixture into dish. In a medium bowl, stir together yogurt, milk, Parmesan cheese, and flour until smooth. Pour evenly over pasta mixture. Sprinkle top with remaining ¼ cup bread crumbs.

3 Bake, covered, for 25 minutes. Uncover and bake for 10 to 15 minutes more until heated through and top is light brown. Let stand for 10 minutes before serving.

Nutrition facts per serving: 425 cal., 15 g total fat (6 g sat. fat), 31 mg chol., 1,045 mg sodium, 57 g carbo., 6 g fiber, 19 g pro.

tortellini AND CHEESE

Boiling the water is the most time-consuming part of making this superfast spin on mac and cheese.

Start to Finish: 20 minutes
Makes: 4 servings

1 9-ounce package refrigerated cheese tortellini
1 cup frozen loose-pack peas, corn, or pea pods
1 8-ounce tub cream cheese spread with garden vegetables or chive and onion
½ cup milk
1 9-ounce package frozen chopped cooked chicken breast

1 Cook tortellini according to package directions. Place frozen vegetables in colander. Drain hot pasta over vegetables to thaw; return pasta-vegetable mixture to hot pan.

2 Meanwhile, in a small saucepan, combine cream cheese and milk; heat and stir until cheese is melted. Heat chicken according to package directions.

3 Stir cream cheese mixture into cooked pasta-vegetable mixture. Cook and gently stir until heated through. Spoon into individual serving bowls. Top with chicken.

Nutrition facts per serving: 505 cal., 26 g total fat (15 g sat. fat), 130 mg chol., 525 mg sodium, 32 g carbo., 2 g fiber, 32 g pro.

creamy MACARONI AND CHEESE

Prep: 20 minutes
Bake: 30 minutes
Stand: 10 minutes
Oven: 350°F
Makes: 6 servings

- **4 slices bacon**
- **1 large sweet onion, thinly sliced**
- **6 ounces dried elbow macaroni**
- **8 ounces mozzarella cheese, shredded (2 cups)**
- **2 to 4 ounces blue cheese, crumbled**
- **1 cup half-and-half or light cream**
- **⅛ teaspoon ground black pepper**

1 Preheat oven to 350°F. In a large skillet, cook bacon over medium heat until crisp, turning once. Drain bacon on paper towels; crumble. Reserve drippings in skillet.

2 Cook onion in reserved drippings for 5 to 8 minutes or until tender and golden brown. Set aside.

3 Cook macaroni according to package directions. Drain; place in a 1½-quart casserole. Add crumbled bacon, onion, 1½ cups of the mozzarella cheese, blue cheese, half-and-half, and pepper. Toss gently to combine.

4 Bake, uncovered, for 20 minutes. Stir gently. Top with remaining mozzarella cheese. Bake for 10 minutes more or until top of casserole is brown and bubbly. Let stand for 10 minutes.

Nutrition facts per serving: 331 cal., 18 g total fat (9 g sat. fat), 45 mg chol., 280 mg sodium, 26 g carbo., 1 g fiber, 16 g pro.

eight-layer CASSEROLE

Prep: 30 minutes
Bake: 55 minutes
Stand: 10 minutes
Chill: up to 24 hours
Makes: 8 servings

3 cups dried medium noodles (6 ounces)

1 pound ground beef

2 8-ounce cans tomato sauce

1 teaspoon dried basil, crushed

½ teaspoon sugar

½ teaspoon garlic powder

¼ teaspoon salt

¼ teaspoon ground black pepper

1 8-ounce carton dairy sour cream

1 8-ounce package cream cheese, softened

½ cup milk

⅓ cup chopped onion (1 small)

1 10-ounce package frozen chopped spinach, cooked and well drained

1 cup shredded cheddar cheese (4 ounces)

1 Preheat oven to 350°F. Cook noodles according to package directions; drain. Set aside. Meanwhile, in a large skillet, cook beef over medium heat until brown. Drain off fat. Stir in tomato sauce, basil, sugar, garlic powder, and salt and pepper. Bring to boiling; reduce heat. Simmer, uncovered, for 5 minutes.

2 In a medium mixing bowl, beat together the sour cream and cream cheese with an electric mixer on medium speed until smooth. Stir in milk and onion. In a greased 2-quart casserole or 2-quart square baking dish, layer half of the noodles (about 2 cups), half of the meat mixture (about 1½ cups), half of the cream cheese mixture (about 1 cup), and all of the spinach. Top with the remaining meat mixture and noodles. Cover and chill remaining cream cheese mixture until needed.

3 Cover casserole with lightly greased foil. Bake for about 45 minutes or until heated through. Uncover; spread remaining cream cheese mixture over top. Sprinkle with the cheddar cheese. Bake, uncovered, for about 10 minutes more or until cheese melts. Let stand for 10 minutes before serving.

Nutrition facts per serving: 472 cal., 30 g total fat (17 g sat. fat), 127 mg chol., 683 mg sodium, 25 g carbo., 3 g fiber, 27 g pro.

To Make Ahead: Cover unbaked casserole with lightly greased foil and refrigerate for up to 24 hours. Bake in a 350°F oven for 1 hour to 1 hour 10 minutes or until heated through. Uncover; spread remaining cream cheese mixture over top. Sprinkle with the cheddar cheese. Bake, uncovered, for about 10 minutes more or until cheese melts. Let stand for 10 minutes before serving.

ravioli SKILLET LASAGNA

Start to Finish: 25 minutes
Makes: 4 servings

- 2 cups purchased chunky-style pasta sauce
- 1/3 cup water
- 1 9-ounce package refrigerated meat or cheese-filled ravioli
- 1 egg, slightly beaten
- 1 15-ounce carton ricotta cheese
- 1/4 cup grated Romano or Parmesan cheese
- 1 10-ounce package frozen chopped spinach, thawed and drained

  Grated Romano or Parmesan cheese

1 In a large skillet, combine pasta sauce and the water. Bring to boiling. Stir in ravioli. Cook, covered, over medium heat for about 5 minutes or until ravioli are nearly tender, stirring once to prevent sticking.

2 In a medium bowl, combine egg, ricotta cheese, and 1/4 cup Romano cheese. Dot ravioli mixture with spinach. Spoon ricotta mixture on top of spinach. Cook, covered, over low heat for about 10 minutes more or until ricotta layer is set and pasta is just tender. Sprinkle with additional grated Romano.

Nutrition facts per serving: 433 cal., 14 g total fat (3 g sat. fat), 131 mg chol., 501 mg sodium, 49 g carbo., 3 g fiber, 36 g pro.

creamy RANCH CHICKEN

Start to Finish: 30 minutes
Makes: 4 servings

6 slices bacon

4 skinless, boneless chicken
   breast halves, cut into bite-
   size pieces

2 tablespoons all-purpose flour

2 tablespoons dry ranch salad
   dressing mix

1¼ cups milk

3 cups dried medium noodles

1 tablespoon finely shredded
   Parmesan cheese

1 Cut bacon into narrow strips. In a large skillet, cook bacon over medium heat until crisp. Drain bacon on paper towels; discard all but 2 tablespoons drippings.

2 In the same skillet, cook chicken in reserved drippings until tender and no longer pink, turning to brown evenly. Sprinkle flour and salad dressing mix over the chicken in the skillet; stir well. Stir in milk. Cook and stir until thickened and bubbly. Cook and stir for 1 minute more. Stir in bacon.

3 Meanwhile, cook noodles according to package directions. Serve chicken mixture with noodles; sprinkle with Parmesan.

Nutrition facts per serving: 488 cal., 18 g total fat (7 g sat. fat), 137 mg chol., 574 mg sodium, 27 g carbo., 1 g fiber, 45 g pro.

chicken AND PASTA IN PEANUT SAUCE

The safest way to cut the chicken breasts in half horizontally is to lay a breast flat on the work surface. Place one hand firmly on top of the chicken, pressing down lightly to hold it steady. Use the other hand to hold the knife horizontally and cut through the meat.

Start to Finish: 20 minutes
Makes: 4 servings

- 8 ounces dried thin spaghetti
- 1 bunch broccolini, cut into 2-inch lengths
- 1 medium red sweet pepper, cut into bite-size strips
- 1 pound skinless, boneless chicken breast halves

    Salt

    Ground black pepper

- 1 tablespoon olive oil
- ½ cup bottled peanut sauce

    Crushed red pepper (optional)

1 In a Dutch oven, cook spaghetti following package directions, adding broccolini and sweet pepper during the last 2 minutes of cooking. Drain. Return pasta and vegetables to Dutch oven; set aside.

2 Meanwhile, halve chicken breasts horizontally. Sprinkle chicken with salt and pepper. In an extra-large skillet, heat olive oil over medium-high heat. Add chicken; cook about 4 minutes or until chicken is no longer pink (170°F), turning once halfway through cooking. Transfer chicken to a cutting board. Slice chicken; add to pasta and vegetables. Heat through. Add peanut sauce. Pass crushed red pepper.

Nutrition facts per serving: 467 cal., 10 g total fat (2 g sat. fat), 66 mg chol., 634 mg sodium, 55 g carbo., 5 g fiber, 37 g pro.

easy CHICKEN POT PIE

Start to Finish: 20 minutes
Oven: 450°F
Makes: 4 servings

½ **cup all-purpose flour**

½ **teaspoon ground sage**

¼ **teaspoon salt**

¼ **teaspoon ground black pepper**

12 **ounces skinless, boneless chicken breast halves**

2 **tablespoons cooking oil**

2 **cups frozen mixed vegetables**

1 **14-ounce can reduced-sodium chicken broth**

½ **cup milk**

1 **11.5-ounce package (8) refrigerated corn bread twists**

½ **cup shredded Mexican cheese blend**

1 Preheat oven to 450°F. In a large resealable plastic bag, combine flour, sage, salt, and pepper. Cut chicken into bite-size pieces. Add chicken to bag; seal bag and shake to coat.

2 In a skillet, brown chicken over medium-high heat for 2 minutes, stirring to brown evenly (chicken will not be completely cooked). In a colander, run cold water over vegetables to thaw. Add vegetables, broth, and milk to skillet. Bring to boiling, stirring once. Divide chicken mixture among four 16-ounce baking dishes.

3 Separate corn bread twists into 16 pieces. Place 4 strips over the chicken mixture in each baking dish. Sprinkle with cheese. Bake for 9 to 10 minutes or until corn bread is brown.

Nutrition facts per serving: 612 cal., 25 g total fat (7 g sat. fat), 64 mg chol., 1,259 mg sodium, 60 g carbo., 3 g fiber, 34 g pro.

turkey AND VEGETABLE BAKE

Rice and vegetables win an encore for the last of the holiday turkey. This creamy main dish gives leftovers a good name.

Prep: 35 minutes
Bake: 30 minutes
Stand: 15 minutes
Oven: 350°F
Makes: 6 servings

2 **cups sliced fresh mushrooms**

¾ **cup chopped red or yellow sweet pepper**

½ **cup chopped onion**

2 **cloves garlic, minced**

2 **tablespoons butter or margarine**

¼ **cup all-purpose flour**

¾ **teaspoon salt**

½ **teaspoon dried thyme, crushed**

¼ **teaspoon ground black pepper**

2 **cups fat-free milk**

1 **10-ounce package frozen chopped spinach, thawed and well drained**

2 **cups cooked brown or white rice**

2 **cups chopped cooked turkey or chicken**

½ **cup finely shredded Parmesan cheese (2 ounces)**

1 Preheat oven to 350°F. In a 12-inch skillet, cook and stir mushrooms, sweet pepper, onion, and garlic in hot butter over medium heat until tender. Stir in flour, salt, thyme, and black pepper. Add milk all at once; cook and stir until thickened and bubbly. Stir in spinach, rice, turkey, and ¼ cup of the Parmesan cheese.

2 Spoon mixture into a 2-quart rectangular baking dish. Sprinkle with remaining Parmesan cheese. Bake, covered, for 20 minutes. Uncover and bake for about 10 minutes more or until heated through. Let stand for 15 minutes before serving.

Nutrition facts per serving: 297 cal., 10 g total fat (5 g sat. fat), 53 mg chol., 602 mg sodium, 28 g carbo., 3 g fiber, 24 g pro.

pork AND NOODLES

Prep: 30 minutes
Chill: 2 to 24 hours
Makes: 8 servings

8 ounces dried Chinese egg
  noodles or fine noodles

1½ pounds fresh asparagus
  spears, trimmed and cut into
  2-inch-long pieces, or one
  16-ounce package frozen cut
  asparagus

4 medium carrots, cut into thin
  ribbons or bite-size strips
  (2 cups)

1 pound cooked lean pork, cut
  into thin strips

  Soy-Sesame Vinaigrette*

  Sesame seeds (optional)

  Sliced green onion (optional)

1 Cook noodles according to package directions; drain. Rinse with cold water until cool; drain.

2 If using fresh asparagus, cook in a covered saucepan in a small amount of lightly salted boiling water for 4 to 6 minutes or until crisp-tender. (Or, if using frozen asparagus, cook according to package directions.) Drain well.

3 In a large bowl, combine noodles, asparagus, carrots, and pork. Cover and chill for 2 to 24 hours.

4 To serve, pour Soy-Sesame Vinaigrette over salad; toss gently to coat. If desired, sprinkle with sesame seeds and green onion.

*Soy-Sesame Vinaigrette: In a screw-top jar, combine ½ cup reduced-sodium soy sauce, ¼ cup rice vinegar or vinegar, ¼ cup honey, 2 tablespoons salad oil, and 2 teaspoons toasted sesame oil. Cover and shake well to mix. Chill for 2 to 24 hours.

Nutrition facts per serving: 338 cal., 12 g total fat (3 g sat. fat), 71 mg chol., 654 mg sodium, 35 g carbo., 3 g fiber, 23 g pro.

easy SHEPHERD'S PIE

Prep: 20 minutes
Bake: 20 minutes
Stand: 10 minutes
Oven: 375°F
Makes: 4 servings

1 17-ounce package refrigerated cooked beef tips with gravy

2 cups frozen mixed vegetables

1 11-ounce can condensed tomato bisque soup

1 tablespoon Worcestershire sauce

1 teaspoon dried minced onion

½ teaspoon dried thyme, crushed

⅛ teaspoon ground black pepper

1 24-ounce package refrigerated mashed potatoes

½ cup shredded cheddar cheese (2 ounces)

1 Preheat oven to 375°F. Lightly grease four 16-ounce individual casserole dishes or a 2-quart square baking dish. In a large saucepan, combine beef tips with gravy, vegetables, soup, Worcestershire sauce, onion, thyme, and pepper. Bring to boiling over medium heat, stirring occasionally. Transfer mixture to prepared baking dishes or dish.

2 In a large bowl, stir potatoes until nearly smooth. Spoon a mound of potatoes onto each individual dish or spoon into six mounds on top of meat mixture in square baking dish.

3 Bake, uncovered, for 20 to 25 minutes or until bubbly around edges. Sprinkle with cheese. Let stand for 10 minutes before serving.

Nutrition facts per serving: 463 cal., 16 g total fat (6 g sat. fat), 65 mg chol., 1,624 mg sodium, 53 g carbo., 6 g fiber, 28 g pro.

Easiest-Ever Beef

When you want a hearty beef dish with slow-simmered flavor but are short on time, open a package of refrigerated cooked beef. Beef roast au jus, beef tips with gravy, and beef pot roast with juices are ready to heat and eat right from the package. They can be the start of a bounty of easy, great-tasting beef dinners.

bean AND BEEF ENCHILADA CASSEROLE

Prep: 25 minutes
Bake: 40 minutes
Chill: up to 24 hours
Makes: 6 servings

½ **pound lean ground beef**

½ **cup chopped onion
    (1 medium)**

1 **teaspoon chili powder**

½ **teaspoon ground cumin**

1 **15-ounce can pinto beans,
    rinsed and drained**

1 **4-ounce can diced green chile
    peppers**

1 **8-ounce carton regular or
    light dairy sour cream**

2 **tablespoons all-purpose flour**

¼ **teaspoon garlic powder**

8 **6-inch corn tortillas**

1 **10-ounce can enchilada
    sauce or one 10.5-ounce can
    tomato puree**

1 **cup shredded cheddar cheese
    (4 ounces)**

1 In a large skillet, cook ground beef, onion, chili powder, and cumin over medium heat until meat is brown. Drain off fat. Stir in beans and undrained chile peppers; set aside. In a small bowl, stir together sour cream, flour, and garlic powder; set aside.

2 Place half of the tortillas in the bottom of a lightly greased 2-quart rectangular baking dish, cutting to fit. Top with half the meat mixture, half the sour cream mixture, half the enchilada sauce, and ½ cup cheese. Repeat layers, except reserve remaining ½ cup cheese. Cover and chill for up to 24 hours.

3 To serve, preheat oven to 350°F. Remove plastic wrap; cover dish with foil. Bake for 35 to 40 minutes or until bubbly. Sprinkle with remaining ½ cup cheese. Bake, uncovered, for about 5 minutes more or until cheese melts.

Nutrition facts per serving: 429 cal., 24 g total fat (12 g sat. fat), 64 mg chol., 632 mg sodium, 36 g carbo., 6 g fiber, 19 g pro.

no-bake TUNA-NOODLE CASSEROLE

Start to Finish: 20 minutes
Makes: 4 servings

8   ounces dried wagon wheel
     pasta or medium shell pasta

¼   to ½ cup milk

1   6.5-ounce container or
     two 4-ounce containers
     light semisoft cheese with
     cucumber and dill or garlic
     and herb

1   12.25-ounce can solid white
     tuna, drained and broken
     into chunks

     Salt

     Ground black pepper

① Cook pasta in lightly salted water according to package directions. Drain and return to pan.

② Add ¼ cup of the milk and the cheese to pasta. Cook and stir over medium heat until cheese melts and pasta is coated, adding milk as needed to make a creamy consistency. Gently fold in tuna; heat through. Season with salt and pepper.

Nutrition facts per serving: 417 cal., 10 g total fat (7 g sat. fat), 66 mg chol., 552 mg sodium, 45 g carbo., 2 g fiber, 33 g pro.

salmon WITH FETA AND PASTA

Feta, the world's favorite Greek cheese, shares its tangy flavor with fish in this colorful combo.

Start to Finish: 25 minutes
Makes: 5 servings

12 ounces fresh or frozen skinless salmon fillet

8 ounces dried rotini

Nonstick cooking spray

1 teaspoon bottled minced garlic

Salt

4 large plum tomatoes, chopped (2 cups)

1 cup sliced green onions

⅓ cup sliced pitted ripe olives

3 tablespoons snipped fresh basil

½ teaspoon coarsely ground black pepper

2 teaspoons olive oil

1 4-ounce package crumbled feta cheese

Fresh basil sprigs (optional)

1 Thaw fish, if frozen. Rinse fish; pat dry with paper towels. Cut into 1-inch pieces. Cook pasta according to package directions. Drain well. Return pasta to hot pan; cover to keep warm.

2 Meanwhile, lightly coat an unheated large nonstick skillet with nonstick cooking spray. Preheat skillet over medium-high heat. Add garlic. Cook and stir for 15 seconds. Lightly season fish pieces with salt. Add fish to skillet. Cook fish for 4 to 6 minutes or until fish flakes easily when tested with a fork, turning fish pieces occasionally. Stir in tomatoes, green onions, olives, basil, and pepper. Heat through.

3 In a large bowl, toss together hot pasta and olive oil. Add salmon mixture and feta cheese; toss gently. If desired, garnish with basil sprigs.

Nutrition facts per serving: 373 cal., 13 g total fat (5 g sat. fat), 56 mg chol., 443 mg sodium, 41 g carbo., 3 g fiber, 24 g pro.

spicy SHRIMP PASTA

Company coming? Stop at the store to pick up the ingredients you probably don't keep on hand: shrimp, chile peppers, and tomatoes. Grab some pasta, bottled minced garlic, oil, salt, and black pepper from your on-hand supply and start cooking.

Start to Finish: 30 minutes
Makes: 4 servings

- 12 ounces fresh or frozen large shrimp in shells
- 8 ounces dried linguine or fettuccine
- 2 tablespoons olive oil or cooking oil
- 1 or 2 fresh jalapeño chile peppers, finely chopped (see tip, page 23)
- 1 teaspoon bottled minced garlic
- ½ teaspoon salt
- ¼ teaspoon ground black pepper
- 2 cups cherry tomatoes, halved
  Finely shredded Parmesan cheese (optional)

1 Thaw shrimp, if frozen. Peel and devein shrimp. Rinse shrimp; pat dry with paper towels. In a large saucepan, cook pasta according to package directions. Drain well. Return pasta to hot pan; cover to keep warm.

2 Meanwhile, in a large skillet, heat oil over medium-high heat. Add chile peppers, garlic, salt, and black pepper; cook and stir for 1 minute. Add shrimp; cook for about 3 minutes more or until shrimp are opaque. Stir in tomatoes; heat through.

3 Toss pasta with shrimp mixture. If desired, pass Parmesan cheese.

Nutrition facts per serving: 363 cal., 9 g total fat (1 g sat. fat), 97 mg chol., 396 mg sodium, 48 g carbo., 3 g fiber, 21 g pro.

red BEANS AND ORZO

Start to Finish: 30 minutes
Makes: 4 servings

 1 **14-ounce can chicken broth**

 1 **cup water**

1½ **cups dried orzo**

 ½ **cup finely chopped onion**

 1 **teaspoon dried Italian
    seasoning, crushed**

 1 **15-ounce can red beans or
    pinto beans, rinsed and
    drained**

 1 **large tomato, peeled, seeded,
    and chopped (1 cup)**

 4 **slices bacon, crisp-cooked and
    crumbled, or ½ cup chopped
    ham**

 ¼ **cup snipped fresh parsley**

 ⅓ **cup finely shredded Parmesan
    cheese**

1 In a large saucepan, bring chicken broth and the water to boiling. Stir in orzo, onion, and Italian seasoning. Reduce heat. Boil gently, uncovered, for 12 to 15 minutes or until orzo is just tender and liquid is absorbed, stirring frequently.

2 Stir in beans, tomato, bacon, and parsley. Heat through. Top each serving with some of the Parmesan cheese.

Nutrition facts per serving: 363 cal., 6 g total fat (2 g sat. fat), 7 mg chol., 800 mg sodium, 59 g carbo., 7 g fiber, 22 g pro.

chipotle TURKEY-STUFFED PEPPERS

Prep: 35 minutes
Bake: 20 minutes + 10 minutes
Stand: 15 minutes
Oven: 425°F/375°F
Makes: 4 servings

- **4 fresh poblano chile peppers or green, red, and/or yellow sweet peppers**
- **12 ounces ground turkey breast or lean ground beef**
- **1⅓ cups cooked brown rice**
- **1 cup purchased roasted tomato salsa**
- **⅓ cup no-salt-added tomato sauce**
- **1 canned chipotle chile pepper in adobo sauce, drained and finely chopped (see tip, page 23)**
- **¼ teaspoon salt**
- **⅓ cup shredded Monterey Jack cheese with jalapeño chile peppers**

❶ Preheat oven to 425°F. Place whole peppers on a foil-lined baking sheet. Bake for 20 to 25 minutes or until skins are blistered and dark. (Or broil 4 to 5 inches from heat for 8 to 10 minutes or until skins are blistered and dark, turning peppers occasionally.) Carefully bring the foil up and around the peppers to enclose. Let stand for about 15 minutes or until cool enough to handle. Pull the skins off gently and slowly using a paring knife. Discard skins. Reduce oven temperature to 375°F.

❷ Cut a thin lengthwise slice from sides of peppers. Remove pepper stems, seeds, and membranes, keeping peppers intact. Place peppers in a 15x10x1-inch baking pan; set aside.

❸ In a large skillet, cook ground turkey over medium heat until brown. Drain off fat. Stir in cooked rice, salsa, tomato sauce, chipotle pepper, and salt; heat through.

❹ Divide turkey mixture among peppers, spooning as much into the cavities as possible and mounding the rest on top of and alongside the peppers. Sprinkle with cheese. Bake for 10 to 15 minutes or until cheese melts and turkey mixture is heated through.

Nutrition facts per serving: 340 cal., 9 g total fat (3 g sat. fat), 45 mg chol., 831 mg sodium, 39 g carbo., 4 g fiber, 28 g pro.

breakfast
AND BREADS

Breakfast Bread Pudding, *recipe page 188*

breakfast TORTILLA WRAP

This bacon-and-egg burrito makes a tidy on-the-go breakfast that you can wrap up in about 10 minutes.

Start to Finish: 10 minutes
Makes: 1 serving

- 1 **slice turkey bacon, chopped**
- 2 **tablespoons chopped green sweet pepper**
- ⅛ **teaspoon ground cumin**
- ⅛ **teaspoon salt (optional)**
- ⅛ **teaspoon crushed red pepper (optional)**
- ¼ **cup refrigerated egg product or 2 slightly beaten egg whites**
- 2 **tablespoons chopped tomato**
- 3 **dashes bottled hot pepper sauce (optional)**
- 1 **8-inch fat-free flour tortilla, warmed**

1 In a medium nonstick skillet, cook bacon until crisp. Add green pepper, cumin, and, if desired, salt and crushed red pepper. Cook for 3 minutes. Add egg product; cook for 2 minutes. Stir in tomato and, if desired, hot pepper sauce. Spoon onto tortilla and roll up.

Nutrition facts per serving: 185 cal., 3 g total fat (1 g sat. fat), 10 mg chol., 643 mg sodium, 27 g carbo., 2 g fiber, 11 g pro.

ham AND POTATO SCRAMBLE

To eliminate some of the chopping, look for packages of diced cooked ham in your supermarket's meat case.

Start to Finish: 25 minutes
Makes: 4 servings

- 8 **eggs**
- ¼ **cup milk**
- ¼ **teaspoon garlic salt**
- ¼ **teaspoon ground black pepper**
- ¼ **cup thinly sliced green onions**
- 1 **tablespoon butter or margarine**
- 1 **cup refrigerated shredded hash brown potatoes**
- ½ **cup diced cooked ham (about 2 ounces)**
- ⅓ **cup shredded cheddar cheese**

1 In a medium bowl, combine eggs, milk, garlic salt, and pepper; beat with a rotary beater or whisk until well mixed. Stir in green onions. Set aside.

2 In a large nonstick skillet, melt butter over medium heat. Add potatoes and ham to skillet; cook for 6 to 8 minutes or until light brown, stirring occasionally. Add egg mixture. Cook over medium heat, without stirring, until mixture begins to set on the bottom and around edge.

3 Using a large spatula, lift and fold the partially cooked egg mixture so the uncooked portion flows underneath. Continue cooking and folding for 2 to 3 minutes more or until egg mixture is cooked through but is still glossy and moist. Remove from heat immediately. Sprinkle with shredded cheese. Serve warm.

Nutrition facts per serving: 289 cal., 18 g total fat (8 g sat. fat), 453 mg chol., 540 mg sodium, 11 g carbo., 1 g fiber, 20 g pro.

quick EGGS BENEDICT

Instead of using the traditional hollandaise sauce, this speedy rendition of the breakfast classic saves time by substituting a seasoned sour cream sauce.

Start to Finish: 20 minutes
Makes: 4 servings

¼ **cup dairy sour cream or crème fraîche**

1 **teaspoon lemon juice**

¾ **to 1 teaspoon dry mustard**

3 **to 4 teaspoons milk**

4 **eggs**

4 **½-inch-thick slices crusty French bread or French bread, lightly toasted**

4 **ounces thinly sliced smoked salmon or 4 slices Canadian-style bacon**

Diced red sweet pepper (optional)

Salt

Ground black pepper

1 In a small bowl, combine sour cream, lemon juice, and dry mustard. Stir in enough of the milk to make desired consistency. Set aside.

2 Lightly grease four cups of an egg poaching pan.* Place the poaching cups over pan of boiling water (water should not touch bottoms of cups); reduce heat to simmering. Break one egg into a measuring cup. Carefully slide egg into a poaching cup. Repeat with remaining eggs. Cover; cook for 6 to 8 minutes or until egg whites are completely set and yolks begin to thicken but are not hard. Run a knife around edges of cups to loosen eggs. Invert poaching cups to remove eggs.

3 Top bread slices with smoked salmon. Top with poached eggs. Top with mustard–sour cream mixture. If desired, sprinkle with sweet pepper. Season to taste with salt and black pepper.

Nutrition facts per serving: 206 cal., 10 g total fat (4 g sat. fat), 225 mg chol., 481 mg sodium, 14 g carbo., 1 g fiber, 14 g pro.

*Test Kitchen Tip: If you don't have an egg poaching pan, lightly grease a 2-quart saucepan with cooking oil or shortening. Fill the pan halfway with water; bring to boiling. Reduce heat to simmering. Break one egg into a measuring cup. Carefully slide egg into water, holding the lip of the cup as close to the water as possible. Repeat with remaining eggs, spacing eggs equally. Simmer, uncovered, for 3 to 5 minutes or until egg whites are completely set and yolks begin to thicken but are not hard. Remove eggs with a slotted spoon.

egg-potato CASSEROLES

Prep: 15 minutes
Bake: 25 minutes
Stand: 5 minutes
Oven: 350°F
Makes: 2 servings

Nonstick cooking spray

⅔ cup frozen loose-pack diced hash brown potatoes with onion and sweet peppers

⅓ cup frozen loose-pack cut broccoli

2 tablespoons chopped Canadian-style bacon or lean cooked ham

2 tablespoons milk

2 teaspoons all-purpose flour

⅔ cup refrigerated or frozen egg product, thawed

3 tablespoons shredded reduced-fat cheddar cheese

1 teaspoon snipped fresh basil or ¼ teaspoon dried basil, crushed

⅛ teaspoon ground black pepper

Pinch salt

1 Preheat oven to 350°F. Lightly coat two 10-ounce casseroles with nonstick cooking spray. Arrange hash brown potatoes and broccoli in casseroles; top with Canadian bacon. In a small bowl, gradually stir milk into flour. Stir in egg, half of the cheese, the basil, pepper, and salt. Pour egg mixture over vegetables.

2 Bake for 25 to 30 minutes or until a knife inserted near the centers comes out clean. Sprinkle with remaining cheese. Let stand for 5 minutes before serving.

Nutrition facts per serving: 171 cal., 4 g total fat (2 g sat. fat), 16 mg chol., 609 mg sodium, 17 g carbo., 1 g fiber, 16 g pro.

mushroom-fontina STRATA

Using mostly egg whites—rather than whole eggs—helps lighten up this strata. If fontina cheese is unavailable, the dish tastes great using part-skim mozzarella cheese or Swiss cheese.

Prep: 25 minutes
Chill: 4 to 24 hours
Bake: 35 minutes
Makes: 6 servings

Nonstick cooking spray

3　cups assorted sliced fresh mushrooms, such as shiitake, white, and/or cremini

½　cup chopped onion

1　clove garlic, minced

2　ounces Canadian-style bacon, finely chopped

8　½-inch-thick slices French bread

½　cup shredded fontina cheese

2　tablespoons assorted snipped fresh herbs (such as basil, oregano, marjoram, or thyme) or 2 teaspoons assorted dried herbs, crushed

1　cup fat-free cottage cheese

1　cup fat-free evaporated milk

3　egg whites

1　egg

1　tablespoon Dijon-style mustard

⅛　teaspoon ground black pepper

1　small tomato, seeded and chopped

1 Spray a medium skillet with nonstick cooking spray. Cook the mushrooms, onion, and garlic in skillet until tender. Drain off any liquid. Stir in Canadian-style bacon.

2 Spray a 2-quart rectangular baking dish with nonstick cooking spray. Arrange the bread slices in the prepared baking dish, cutting as necessary to fit. Sprinkle mushroom mixture over bread. In a small bowl, toss together fontina cheese and desired herbs. Sprinkle over mushroom mixture.

3 In a blender container or food processor bowl combine cottage cheese, evaporated milk, egg whites, egg, mustard, and pepper. Cover and blend or process until smooth; pour evenly over ingredients in baking dish. Lightly press bread down with the back of a spoon. Cover; chill for 4 to 24 hours.

4 Preheat oven to 350°F. Bake, uncovered, for about 35 minutes or until a knife inserted near the center comes out clean. Sprinkle with chopped tomato. Let stand for 5 minutes before serving.

Nutrition facts per serving: 227 cal., 6 g total fat (2 g sat. fat), 56 mg chol., 543 mg sodium, 24 g carbo., 1 g fiber, 20 g pro.

turkey SAUSAGE STRATA

Prep: 25 minutes
Chill: 6 to 24 hours
Bake: 1 hour
Oven: 325°F
Makes: 12 servings

- **1 pound bulk turkey sausage**
- **½ cup chopped onion (1 medium)**
- **12 slices white bread**
- **1 9-ounce package frozen cut broccoli, thawed and well drained**
- **1 cup shredded mozzarella cheese (4 ounces)**
- **1 2-ounce jar sliced pimiento, drained**
- **6 eggs, beaten**
- **3 cups milk**
- **½ teaspoon salt**
- **¼ teaspoon dry mustard**

1 In a medium skillet, cook sausage and onion over medium heat until meat is brown. Drain off fat. In a greased 3-quart rectangular baking dish, layer six slices bread, half the sausage mixture, half the broccoli, half the mozzarella, and half the pimiento. Repeat layers.

2 In a bowl, combine beaten eggs, milk, salt, and dry mustard. Pour over the layers in the dish. Cover; chill for 6 to 24 hours.

3 Preheat oven to 325°F. Bake, uncovered, for 1 hour or until a knife inserted near center comes out clean.

Nutrition facts per serving: 238 cal., 11 g total fat (4 g sat. fat), 146 mg chol., 639 mg sodium, 19 g carbo., 1 g fiber, 17 g pro.

beef hash WITH A SPICY KICK

Prep: 30 minutes
Marinate: 30 minutes
Cook: 20 minutes
Makes: 6 servings

½ cup orange juice

2 tablespoons lime juice

1 tablespoon adobo sauce (from canned chipotle chile peppers)

1¼ pounds beef sirloin or top loin steak, finely chopped

2 large onions, chopped (2 cups)

2 tablespoons minced garlic or bottled minced garlic

1 tablespoon chili powder

1 tablespoon cooking oil

1½ pounds Yukon gold potatoes or red potatoes, cooked and diced

1 tablespoon chopped chipotle chile peppers in adobo sauce

2 roma tomatoes, seeded and chopped

¼ cup snipped fresh cilantro

Salt

Ground black pepper

Fried eggs (optional)

Fresh cilantro sprigs (optional)

1 In a plastic bag set in a bowl, combine orange juice, lime juice, and adobo sauce; add meat, turning to coat. Seal bag. Marinate in refrigerator for 30 minutes. Drain and discard marinade. Pat meat dry with paper towels.

2 In a 12-inch heavy skillet, cook onions, garlic, and chili powder in hot oil over medium heat for 5 minutes or until onion is tender. Increase heat to medium-high. Add meat to skillet; cook and stir for about 2 minutes or until meat is brown. Stir in potatoes and chipotle peppers. Spread in an even layer in the skillet. Cook for about 8 minutes more or until potatoes are golden brown, turning occasionally. Fold in tomatoes and cilantro; heat through. Season with salt and black pepper. If desired, serve with fried eggs and garnish with fresh cilantro.

Nutrition facts per serving: 263 cal., 6 g total fat (2 g sat. fat), 45 mg chol., 189 mg sodium, 28 g carbo., 4 g fiber, 24 g pro.

banana-pecan WAFFLES

The waffles are done when steam stops escaping from the sides of the baker or when the indicator light comes on.

Prep: 20 minutes
Cook: 3 to 4 minutes per waffle
Makes: about 9 waffles

1¾ cups all-purpose flour

2 tablespoons sugar

1 tablespoon baking powder

½ teaspoon ground cinnamon

¼ teaspoon salt

2 small bananas, mashed (¾ cup)

2 eggs

1 cup milk

¼ cup cooking oil or melted butter

1 teaspoon vanilla

½ cup finely chopped pecans, toasted and cooled

Butter, maple syrup, caramel ice cream topping, sliced bananas, and/or chopped toasted pecans (optional)

❶ In a large bowl, stir together flour, sugar, baking powder, cinnamon, and salt.

❷ In medium bowl, beat together banana and eggs. Stir in milk, cooking oil, and vanilla. Add banana mixture all at once to the flour mixture. Stir just until moistened (batter should be slightly lumpy). Stir in ½ cup pecans.

❸ Add batter to a preheated, lightly greased waffle baker according to manufacturer's directions. Close lid quickly; do not open until done. Bake according to manufacturer's directions. When done, use a fork to lift waffle off grid. Repeat with remaining batter. Serve warm* with desired toppings.

Nutrition facts per serving: 241 cal., 12 g total fat (2 g sat. fat), 49 mg chol., 172 mg sodium, 28 g carbo., 2 g fiber, 5 g pro.

*Test Kitchen Tip: Keep prepared waffles warm in a 300°F oven while baking the other waffles.

pancakes WITH BERRY SAUCE

A fresh strawberry sauce drizzled over feathery-light whole wheat pancakes is sure to open sleepy eyes.

Start to Finish: 25 minutes
Makes: 5 (2-pancake) servings

- ½ **cup whole wheat flour**
- ½ **cup all-purpose flour**
- 1 **tablespoon sugar**
- 2 **teaspoons baking powder**
- ¼ **teaspoon salt**
- ¾ **cup fat-free milk**
- 1 **teaspoon cooking oil**
- 2 **egg whites**
  Nonstick cooking spray
- 2 **cups fresh or frozen unsweetened strawberries, thawed**
- 1 **tablespoon sugar**
- 1 **teaspoon vanilla**
  Quartered fresh strawberries (optional)

1 In a medium bowl, combine whole wheat flour, all-purpose flour, sugar, baking powder, and salt. Stir in milk and oil. In another bowl, beat egg whites until stiff (tips stand straight). Fold egg whites into flour mixture.

2 Lightly coat a griddle with nonstick cooking spray. Heat griddle over medium heat. For each pancake, pour about ¼ cup batter onto the hot griddle. Cook over medium heat until pancakes are golden brown (1 to 2 minutes per side); turn to second sides when pancakes have bubbly surfaces and slightly dry edges.

3 Meanwhile, in a blender container or food processor bowl, combine strawberries, sugar, and vanilla. Cover and blend or process until smooth. In a small saucepan, heat sauce until warm. If desired, top pancakes with quartered strawberries. Serve pancakes with sauce.

Nutrition facts per serving: 148 cal., 2 g total fat, 1 mg chol., 319 mg sodium, 28 g carbo., 3 g fiber, 6 g pro.

apple BUTTER HOTCAKES

Prep: 25 minutes
Cook: 4 minutes per batch
Makes: 8 to 10 hotcakes

½ **cup butter, softened**
¼ **cup honey**
¼ **teaspoon ground cinnamon**
1 **12-ounce package frozen pitted light or dark sweet cherries**
½ **cup cherry jam or cherry preserves**
1 **teaspoon finely shredded orange peel**
1½ **cups packaged regular or buttermilk pancake mix**
¾ **cup milk**
2 **tablespoons cooking oil**
2 **eggs, lightly beaten**
½ **cup purchased apple butter**

1 For flavored butter, in a small mixing bowl, whisk together butter, honey, and cinnamon; set aside.

2 For cherry sauce, in a medium saucepan, combine frozen cherries, cherry jam, and orange peel. Bring to boiling over medium heat, stirring frequently; reduce heat. Simmer, uncovered, for 10 minutes or until sauce has thickened slightly. Cover and set aside; keep warm.

3 In a medium bowl, stir together pancake mix, milk, oil, eggs, and apple butter. Stir just until moistened (batter should still be lumpy). On a hot lightly greased griddle, spread about ¼ cup batter into a 4-inch circle. Cook over medium heat for about 2 minutes on each side or until hot cakes are golden brown, turning to second sides when hot cakes have bubbly surfaces and edges are slightly dry. Serve warm with butter and sauce.

Nutrition facts per hotcake: 456 cal., 16 g total fat (8 g sat. fat), 84 mg chol., 400 mg sodium, 72 g carbo., 4 g fiber, 4 g pro.

oat PANCAKES

Pancakes always are a treat for a leisurely weekend breakfast or brunch. But these wheat and oat pancakes are exceptionally good. The pear sauce with a hint of maple adds the crowning touch.

Prep: 30 minutes
Stand: 15 to 30 minutes
Cook: 4 minutes per batch
Makes: 8 (¼-cup) servings

1¼ cups regular rolled oats

¾ cup all-purpose flour

½ cup whole wheat flour

1 tablespoon baking powder

¼ teaspoon salt

3 egg whites, slightly beaten

2¼ cups buttermilk

2 tablespoons cooking oil

2 tablespoons honey (optional)

1 teaspoon vanilla

Maple-Pear Sauce*

Nonstick cooking spray

① In a large bowl, combine the oats, all-purpose flour, whole wheat flour, baking powder, and salt. Make a well in the center of mixture; set aside. In a medium bowl, combine the egg whites, buttermilk, oil, honey (if desired), and vanilla. Add egg white mixture all at once to flour mixture. Stir just until moistened (batter should be lumpy). Cover batter; allow to stand at room temperature for 15 to 30 minutes. Meanwhile, prepare Maple-Pear Sauce; keep warm.

② Spray a griddle or heavy skillet with nonstick cooking spray. Preheat over medium-high heat. For each pancake, pour about ¼ cup of the batter onto the hot griddle or skillet. Spread batter into a circle about 4 inches in diameter. Cook over medium heat for about 2 minutes on each side or until the pancakes are golden, turning to cook second sides when pancakes have bubbly surfaces and edges are slightly dry. Serve with Maple-Pear Sauce.

***Maple-Pear Sauce:** Peel and core 4 large pears; cut pears into ¼-inch slices. Toss with 1 tablespoon lemon juice; set aside. In a large heavy saucepan, combine ½ cup unsweetened apple juice, ½ cup sugar-free pancake and waffle syrup product, and 3 inches stick cinnamon. Bring to boiling. Add pear slices; reduce heat. Simmer, uncovered, for 3 to 5 minutes or until the pears are tender. Stir together 2 tablespoons unsweetened apple juice and 1 tablespoon cornstarch; stir into pear mixture along with ¼ cup dried cranberries. Cook and stir until bubbly. Cook and stir for 2 minutes more. Remove from heat and discard cinnamon.

Nutrition facts per serving: 257 cal., 5 g total fat (1 g sat. fat), 3 mg chol., 320 mg sodium, 46 g carbo., 3 g fiber, 8 g pro.

stuffed FRENCH TOAST

The cream cheese and fruit stuffing creates a delicious surprise with every bite. To save time in the morning, fill the pockets the night before, covering the bread tightly with plastic wrap and storing it in the refrigerator.

Prep: 15 minutes
Bake: 8 minutes
Makes: 4 servings

4 **1-inch-thick diagonally cut slices French bread**

¼ **of an 8-ounce tub light cream cheese**

½ **cup finely chopped fruit, such as nectarines or peeled peaches, pears, or apricots**

1 **teaspoon sugar-free apricot, apricot-pineapple, orange marmalade, or peach spread**

Nonstick cooking spray

¼ **cup refrigerated or frozen egg product, thawed**

¼ **cup fat-free milk**

⅛ **teaspoon ground cinnamon**

½ **cup sugar-free apricot, apricot-pineapple, orange marmalade, or peach spread**

1 Preheat oven to 450°F. Cut a pocket in the top of each bread slice; set aside. In a small bowl, stir together the cream cheese, chopped fruit, and the 1 teaspoon fruit spread. Fill each pocket with a rounded tablespoon of the cream cheese mixture.

2 Spray a foil-lined baking sheet with nonstick cooking spray; set aside. In a shallow bowl, stir together the egg product, milk, and cinnamon. Dip the stuffed slices into the egg mixture, coating both sides.

3 Arrange bread slices on the prepared baking sheet. Bake for 8 to 10 minutes or until heated through.

4 Meanwhile, in a small saucepan heat the remaining ½ cup fruit spread over medium heat just until melted. Invert the French toast onto serving plates. Top with melted spread.

Nutrition facts per serving: 196 cal., 6 g total fat (1 g sat. fat), 18 mg chol., 355 mg sodium, 28 g carbo., 0 g fiber, 6 g pro.

streusel FRENCH TOAST

Crushed, shredded wheat biscuits add a slightly crunchy topping to this make-ahead, nutrition-packed breakfast. Fresh strawberries make it even more special.

Prep: 20 minutes
Chill: 2 to 24 hours
Bake: 30 minutes
Makes: 6 servings

Nonstick cooking spray

¾ **cup refrigerated or frozen egg product, thawed, or 3 eggs, slightly beaten**

1 **cup evaporated fat-free milk**

3 **tablespoons sugar**

2 **teaspoons vanilla**

½ **teaspoon ground cinnamon**

¼ **teaspoon ground nutmeg**

6 **1-inch slices Italian bread (3 to 4 inches in diameter)**

1 **large shredded wheat biscuit, crushed (⅔ cup)**

1 **tablespoon butter or margarine, melted**

2 **cups sliced strawberries**

3 **tablespoons sugar, or sugar substitute equal to 3 tablespoons sugar**

½ **teaspoon ground cinnamon**

❶ Spray a 2-quart rectangular baking dish with nonstick coating; set aside. In a medium bowl, beat together the egg product or eggs, evaporated milk, 3 tablespoons sugar, vanilla, ½ teaspoon cinnamon, and nutmeg. Arrange the bread slices in a single layer in prepared baking dish. Pour egg mixture evenly over slices. Cover and chill for 2 to 24 hours, turning bread slices once with a wide spatula.

❷ Preheat oven to 375°F. Combine crushed biscuit and melted butter or margarine; sprinkle evenly over the bread slices. Bake, uncovered, for about 30 minutes until lightly browned.

❸ Meanwhile, in a small bowl combine the strawberries, 3 tablespoons sugar or sugar substitute, and ½ teaspoon cinnamon. Serve with French toast.

Nutrition facts per serving: 244 cal., 5 g total fat (2 g sat. fat), 7 mg chol., 300 mg sodium, 41 g carbo., 1 g fiber, 10 g pro.

breakfast BREAD PUDDING

If you love bread pudding, here's a great way to start the day. Cubes of cinnamon-swirl bread nestle in a custard made with protein-packed egg product and fat-free milk.

Prep: 25 minutes
Bake: 35 minutes
Stand: 15 minutes
Oven: 325°F
Makes: 6 servings

6 slices cinnamon-swirl bread
   or cinnamon-raisin bread

   Nonstick cooking spray

1½ cups fat-free milk

¾ cup refrigerated or frozen
   egg product, thawed

3 tablespoons sugar

1 teaspoon vanilla

¼ teaspoon ground nutmeg

1 5.5-ounce can apricot or
   peach nectar (⅔ cup)

2 teaspoons cornstarch

1 Preheat oven to 325°F. To dry bread, place slices in a single layer on a baking sheet. Bake for 10 minutes, turning once. Cool on a wire rack. Cut slices into ½-inch cubes (you should have about 4 cups).

2 Lightly coat six 6-ounce soufflé dishes or custard cups with nonstick cooking spray. Divide bread cubes among the prepared dishes. In a medium bowl, combine milk, egg product, sugar, vanilla, and nutmeg. Use a rotary beater or wire whisk to beat until mixed. Pour milk mixture evenly over bread cubes. Press lightly with the back of a spoon to thoroughly moisten bread.

3 Place dishes in a 13x9x2-inch baking pan. Place baking pan on oven rack. Carefully pour the hottest tap water available into the baking pan around dishes to a depth of 1 inch.

4 Bake in the 325°F oven for 35 to 40 minutes or until a knife inserted near centers comes out clean. Transfer dishes to a wire rack. Let stand for 15 to 20 minutes.

5 Meanwhile, for sauce, in a small saucepan gradually stir apricot nectar into cornstarch. Cook and stir over medium heat until thickened and bubbly. Reduce heat. Cook and stir for 2 minutes more. Spoon sauce over warm puddings.

Nutrition facts per serving: 164 cal., 2 g total fat (1 g sat. fat), 1 mg chol., 189 mg sodium, 28 g carbo., 0 g fiber, 8 g pro.

tropical COFFEE CAKE

Mango and coconut give this delicious coffee cake an island flair. Yogurt and just a small amount of oil help keep the cake moist. If you can't find mangoes, substitute nectarines or peaches.

Prep: 25 minutes
Bake: 35 minutes
Makes: 8 servings

1¼ **cups all-purpose flour**

¼ **cup sugar plus 4 packets heat-stable sugar substitute, or ½ cup sugar**

½ **teaspoon baking powder**

½ **teaspoon baking soda**

¼ **teaspoon salt**

¼ **teaspoon ground nutmeg**

1 **egg, beaten**

⅔ **cup fat-free plain yogurt**

2 **tablespoons cooking oil**

½ **teaspoon vanilla**

1 **medium mango, peeled, seeded, and finely chopped (about 1 cup)**

1 **tablespoon all-purpose flour**

2 **tablespoons flaked coconut**

1 Preheat oven to 350°F. Lightly grease and flour a 9x1½-inch round baking pan; set aside. In a large bowl, stir together the 1¼ cups flour, the sugar plus sugar substitute or the sugar, baking powder, baking soda, salt, and nutmeg. Make a well in the center of the flour mixture.

2 In a small mixing bowl, stir together the egg, yogurt, oil, and vanilla. Add the egg mixture all at once to flour mixture. Stir just until moistened (batter should be slightly lumpy). Toss chopped mango with the 1 tablespoon flour; gently fold into batter. Spread batter into prepared pan.

3 Sprinkle coconut over batter in pan. Bake for 35 minutes. Serve warm.

Nutrition facts per serving: 169 cal., 5 g total fat (1 g sat. fat), 27 mg chol., 194 mg sodium, 28 g carbo., 1 g fiber, 4 g pro.

bananas FOSTER OATMEAL

For a breakfast that's quick to make and keeps you going all morning long, add banana slices, toasted pecans, and caramel ice cream topping to a packet of instant oatmeal.

Start to Finish: 10 minutes
Makes: 2 servings

2 **1-ounce envelopes instant oatmeal (plain)**

1 **medium banana, sliced**

2 **tablespoons chopped pecans, toasted**

2 **to 3 teaspoons caramel ice cream topping**

Fat-free milk (optional)

❶ In two microwave-safe bowls, prepare oatmeal according to package directions. Top with banana and pecans. Drizzle with caramel topping.

❷ If desired, microwave on 100% power (high) for about 30 seconds or until toppings are warm. If desired, serve with fat-free milk.

Nutrition facts per serving: 230 cal., 7 g total fat (1 g sat. fat), 0 mg chol., 17 mg sodium, 38 g carbo., 5 g fiber, 6 g pro.

fruited GRANOLA

This very berry granola starts your day with an appetizing crunch. Bowls of the cinnamon-scented cereal make great snacks too.

Prep: 15 minutes
Bake: 38 minutes
Oven: 325°F
Makes: 5 servings

Nonstick cooking spray

2½ **cups regular rolled oats**

 1 **cup whole bran cereal**

 ½ **cup toasted wheat germ**

 ¼ **cup sliced almonds**

 ½ **cup raspberry applesauce**

 ⅓ **cup honey**

 ¼ **teaspoon ground cinnamon**

 ⅓ **cup dried cranberries, blueberries, and/or cherries**

Vanilla low-fat yogurt or fat-free milk (optional)

1 Preheat oven to 325°F. Lightly coat a 15x10x1-inch baking pan with nonstick cooking spray; set aside. In a large bowl, stir together rolled oats, bran cereal, wheat germ, and almonds. In a small bowl, stir together applesauce, honey, and cinnamon. Pour applesauce mixture over cereal mixture; stir until combined.

2 Spread cereal mixture evenly in the prepared baking pan. Bake for 35 minutes, stirring occasionally. Carefully stir in dried cranberries. Bake for 3 to 5 minutes more or until golden brown.

3 Turn out onto a large piece of foil to cool completely. To store, place in an airtight container for up to 2 weeks. If desired, serve with vanilla yogurt or fat-free milk.

Nutrition facts per serving: 216 cal., 4 g total fat (1 g sat. fat), 0 mg chol., 18 mg sodium, 41 g carbo., 6 g fiber, 7 g pro.

blueberry BREAKFAST SCONES

Spread good morning cheer with these orange-glazed scones served warm with a dab of butter.

Prep: 25 minutes
Bake: 15 minutes
Oven: 400°F
Makes: 10 scones

- 2   **cups all-purpose flour**
- ¼   **cup sugar**
- 1   **tablespoon baking powder**
- 1   **tablespoon finely shredded orange peel**
- ¼   **teaspoon salt**
- ¼   **teaspoon baking soda**
- ¼   **cup butter**
- ½   **cup buttermilk or sour milk****
- ¼   **cup refrigerated or frozen egg product, thawed**
- 1   **teaspoon vanilla**
- 1   **cup fresh or frozen blueberries**
-     **Nonstick cooking spray**
-     **Orange Powdered Sugar Icing***

1 Preheat oven to 400°F. In a large bowl, stir together flour, sugar, baking powder, orange peel, salt, and baking soda. Using a pastry blender, cut in butter until mixture resembles coarse crumbs. Make a well in the center of the flour mixture. Combine buttermilk, egg product, and vanilla. Add to flour mixture all at once, stirring just until moistened. Gently stir in blueberries. Lightly coat a baking sheet with nonstick cooking spray; set aside.

2 Turn dough out onto a lightly floured surface. Quickly knead dough by folding and pressing gently for 12 to 15 strokes or until nearly smooth. Pat dough into a 7-inch circle on the prepared baking sheet. Cut dough into 10 wedges.

3 Bake for 15 to 20 minutes or until golden brown. Cool slightly on a wire rack. Drizzle Orange Powdered Sugar Icing over tops of scones.

*Orange Powdered Sugar Icing: In a small bowl, stir together ¾ cup sifted powdered sugar and ¼ teaspoon finely shredded orange peel. Stir in enough orange juice or fat-free milk (3 to 4 teaspoons) to make an icing of drizzling consistency.

Nutrition facts per scone: 194 cal., 5 g total fat (3 g sat. fat), 13 mg chol., 273 mg sodium, 34 g carbo., 1 g fiber, 4 g pro.

**Note: To make ½ cup sour milk, place 1½ teaspoons lemon juice or vinegar in a glass measuring cup. Add enough fat-free milk to make ½ cup total liquid; stir. Let stand for 5 minutes before using.

pumpkin MUFFINS

The secret to these enticing muffins is a combination of moist, rich pumpkin and flavorful buckwheat. Though buckwheat is often thought of as a cereal, it actually is made from the seeds of the buckwheat herb.

Prep: 20 minutes
Bake: 15 minutes
Makes: 12 muffins

Nonstick cooking spray
1⅓ **cups all-purpose flour**
¾ **cup buckwheat flour**
¼ **cup sugar plus 2 packets heat-stable sugar substitute, or ⅓ cup sugar**
1½ **teaspoons baking powder**
1 **teaspoon ground cinnamon**
½ **teaspoon baking soda**
½ **teaspoon salt**
2 **eggs, slightly beaten**
1 **cup canned pumpkin**
½ **cup fat-free milk**
2 **tablespoons cooking oil**
½ **teaspoon finely shredded orange peel**
¼ **cup orange juice**

1 Preheat oven to 400°F. Spray twelve 2½-inch muffin cups with nonstick coating; set pan aside. In a medium bowl combine the all-purpose flour, buckwheat flour, sugar plus sugar substitute or the sugar, baking powder, cinnamon, baking soda, and salt. Make a well in the center of flour mixture; set aside.

2 In another bowl, combine the eggs, pumpkin, milk, oil, orange peel, and orange juice. Add the egg mixture all at once to the flour mixture. Stir just until moistened (batter should be lumpy).

3 Spoon batter into the prepared muffin cups, dividing the batter evenly. Bake for 15 to 20 minutes or until the muffins are light brown. Cool in muffin cups on a wire rack for 5 minutes. Remove from muffin cups; serve warm.

Nutrition facts per muffin: 134 cal., 4 g total fat (1 g sat. fat), 36 mg chol., 204 mg sodium, 22 g carbo., 2 g fiber, 4 g pro.

apple-cheddar MUFFINS

Applesauce and dried fruit keep these muffins moist. Spicy and aromatic, they're good for breakfast, brunch, tea, or snacks—especially when served with a cup of tea, cold milk, or hot cider.

Prep: 20 minutes
Bake: 20 minutes
Makes: 12 muffins

Nonstick cooking spray

1¼ **cups unprocessed wheat bran (Miller's Bran)**

1 **cup all-purpose flour**

½ **cup shredded reduced-fat sharp cheddar cheese (2 ounces)**

2 **teaspoons baking powder**

½ **teaspoon ground cinnamon**

¼ **teaspoon baking soda**

¼ **teaspoon salt**

¾ **cup unsweetened applesauce**

½ **cup fat-free milk**

3 **tablespoons honey plus 2 packets heat-stable sugar substitute, or ⅓ cup honey**

¼ **cup refrigerated or frozen egg product, thawed**

1 **tablespoon cooking oil**

½ **cup finely snipped dried apples or raisins**

1 Preheat oven to 400°F. Spray twelve 2½-inch muffin cups with nonstick cooking spray; set aside. In a medium bowl, combine wheat bran, flour, cheese, baking powder, cinnamon, baking soda, and salt. Make a well in the center of the flour mixture; set aside.

2 In another bowl, combine applesauce, milk, honey plus sugar substitute or honey, egg product, and oil. Add applesauce mixture all at once to flour mixture. Stir just until moistened (batter should be lumpy). Fold in dried apples or raisins.

3 Spoon the batter into prepared muffin cups, filling each three-quarters full. Bake for about 20 minutes or until golden. Cool in muffin cups on a wire rack for 5 minutes. Remove from muffin cups; serve warm.

Nutrition facts per muffin: 114 cal., 3 g total fat (1 g sat. fat), 4 mg chol., 184 mg sodium, 21 g carbo., 2 g fiber, 4 g pro.

pear-almond MUFFINS

Cream cheese laced with ginger and honey complements these fruit-filled muffins. Store the batter in the refrigerator for up to 3 days and bake a few at a time, if you like.

Prep: 20 minutes
Bake: 15 minutes
Stand: 10 minutes
Oven: 400°F
Makes: 7 muffins

Nonstick cooking spray
⅔ **cup all-purpose flour**
⅓ **cup packed brown sugar**
1½ **teaspoons baking powder**
¼ **teaspoon ground ginger**
⅛ **teaspoon salt**
½ **cup whole bran cereal**
½ **cup fat-free milk**
½ **cup chopped, peeled pear**
2 **tablespoons refrigerated or frozen egg product, thawed**
2 **tablespoons cooking oil**
1 **tablespoon finely chopped**

1 Lightly coat 7 muffin cups with nonstick cooking spray or line with paper baking cups; set aside. In a medium bowl stir together flour, brown sugar, baking powder, ginger, and salt. Make a well in the center of the flour mixture; set aside.

2 In another medium bowl stir together cereal and milk; let cereal mixture stand for 5 minutes. Stir in pear, egg product, and oil. Add cereal mixture all at once to flour mixture. Stir just until moistened (batter should be lumpy). (If desired, cover and refrigerate the batter in an airtight container for up to 3 days. Bake muffins as needed.)

3 Spoon batter into prepared muffin cups, filling each three-fourths full. Sprinkle with nuts.

4 Bake in a 400°F oven for 15 to 18 minutes or until a wooden toothpick inserted near centers comes out clean. Cool in muffin cups on a wire rack for 5 minutes. Remove from muffin cups. Serve warm with Ginger-Cream Spread.

Ginger-Cream Spread: In a small bowl stir together one-third of an 8-ounce tub fat-free cream cheese, 1½ teaspoons honey, and 1½ teaspoons finely chopped crystallized ginger or ⅛ teaspoon ground ginger.

Nutrition facts per muffin: 165 cal., 5 g total fat (1 g sat. fat), 2 mg chol., 157 mg sodium, 28 g carbo., 2 g fiber, 5 g pro.

wheat AND OAT BREAD

Even a novice bread baker can succeed with this quick bread. The loaf has a crunchy wheat germ–topped crust and a pleasing nutty flavor. Warm from the oven, this bread is irresistible.

Prep: 20 minutes
Bake: 35 minutes
Makes: 16 servings

Nonstick cooking spray

1¾ cups all-purpose flour

¾ cup whole wheat flour

½ cup regular rolled oats, toasted*

3 tablespoons toasted wheat germ

3 tablespoons sugar

2½ teaspoons baking powder

¼ teaspoon salt

1⅓ cups fat-free milk

¼ cup refrigerated or frozen egg product, thawed

2 tablespoons cooking oil

1 tablespoon toasted wheat germ

1 Preheat oven to 375°F. Spray the bottom and sides of an 8x1½-inch round baking pan with nonstick cooking spray; set aside.

2 In a large bowl, stir together the all-purpose flour, whole wheat flour, toasted oats, the 3 tablespoons wheat germ, sugar, baking powder, and salt. In another bowl, combine milk, egg product, and oil. Add milk mixture all at once to dry mixture. Stir just until moistened (batter should be lumpy). Spread batter in prepared pan. Sprinkle with the 1 tablespoon wheat germ.

3 Bake for 35 to 40 minutes or until golden brown and a toothpick inserted near the center comes out clean. Cool bread in pan on a wire rack for 10 minutes. Remove from pan; serve warm.

*Note: To toast rolled oats, place in a shallow baking pan. Bake rolled oats in a 350°F oven for 5 to 8 minutes or until oats are lightly browned, shaking pan once.

Nutrition facts per serving: 116 cal., 3 g total fat (0 g sat. fat), 0 mg chol., 108 mg sodium, 20 g carbo., 1 g fiber, 4 g pro.

A Germ to Behold

Wheat germ—the toasted and ground "germ" of the wheat kernel—is concentrated in protein and minerals. Toasted wheat germ perks up cereals or soups and brings texture to baked goods. It even can bring its nutlike flavor to sandwich spreads—try folding a teaspoon or two into chicken or tuna salad. Look for toasted wheat germ in health food stores and most supermarkets.

whole WHEAT POPOVERS

Steam causes the batter to rise and "pop over" the sides of the baking cups. For moist popovers, remove from the oven immediately after baking; for crisper results, turn off the oven and let "bake" for a few more minutes.

Prep: 20 minutes
Bake: 40 minutes
Makes: 6 popovers

Nonstick cooking spray

2 **eggs, beaten**
1 **cup fat-free milk**
1 **teaspoon cooking oil**
¾ **cup all-purpose flour**
¼ **cup whole wheat flour**
¼ **teaspoon salt**

1 Preheat oven to 400°F. Spray bottoms and sides of six 6-ounce custard cups or cups of a popover pan with nonstick cooking spray. Set aside.

2 In a mixing bowl, use a wire whisk or rotary beater to beat eggs, milk, and oil until combined. Add all-purpose flour, whole wheat flour, and salt; beat until smooth. Fill prepared cups half full with batter.

3 Bake for about 40 minutes or until very firm. Immediately after removing from oven, prick each popover to allow the steam to escape. (For crisper popovers, turn off the oven; return the popovers to the oven for 5 to 10 minutes or until desired crispness is reached.) Remove popovers from cups; serve immediately.

Nutrition facts per popover: 119 cal., 3 g total fat (1 g sat. fat), 73 mg chol., 131 mg sodium, 17 g carbo., 1 g fiber, 6 g pro.

tomato-basil CORN BREAD

Enjoy old-fashioned corn bread with a new twist! This updated classic has fewer calories and less fat than the original, but the flavor is better than ever due to the addition of basil and zesty dried tomatoes.

Prep: 20 minutes
Bake: 15 minutes
Makes: 12 servings

Nonstick cooking spray

1 cup all-purpose flour

1 cup cornmeal

2 tablespoons sugar

2 tablespoons snipped fresh basil or 1 teaspoon dried basil, crushed

1 tablespoon baking powder

¼ teaspoon salt

1 cup fat-free milk

½ cup refrigerated egg product

3 tablespoons cooking oil

½ cup dried tomato pieces (not oil-packed)

1 Preheat oven to 425°F. Spray a 9x1½-inch round baking pan with nonstick cooking spray; set aside. In a large bowl combine flour, cornmeal, sugar, basil, baking powder, and salt. In small bowl combine the milk, egg product, and oil. Add the milk mixture all at once to flour mixture. Stir just until moistened (batter should be lumpy). Fold the tomato pieces into the batter. Spoon the batter into prepared pan.

2 Bake for 15 to 20 minutes or until a wooden toothpick inserted into center comes out clean. Cool on a wire rack. Cut into wedges to serve.

Nutrition facts per serving: 138 cal., 4 g total fat (1 g sat. fat), 0 mg chol., 212 mg sodium, 21 g carbo., 1 g fiber, 4 g pro.

chile AND CHEESE CORN BREAD

Want to be hailed as the hero of the kitchen? Just serve chunks of this pepper-, corn-, and onion-laced corn bread. It's the ideal accompaniment for hot soup, grilled meat, or baked chicken.

Prep: 25 minutes
Bake: 20 minutes
Makes: 18 servings

Nonstick cooking spray

1 **tablespoon margarine or butter**

⅓ **cup finely chopped red sweet pepper**

¼ **cup finely chopped red onion**

⅔ **cup whole kernel corn**

3 **tablespoons canned diced green chile peppers, drained**

1⅓ **cups yellow cornmeal**

1¼ **cups all-purpose flour**

2 **teaspoons baking powder**

1 **teaspoon sugar**

½ **teaspoon baking soda**

¼ **teaspoon salt**

1¼ **cups buttermilk**

2 **eggs, slightly beaten**

2 **tablespoons margarine or butter, melted and cooled**

½ **cup shredded, reduced-fat cheddar cheese**

1 Preheat oven to 425°F. Spray an 11x7x2-inch baking pan with nonstick cooking spray; set aside. In a medium skillet heat the 1 tablespoon margarine or butter over medium-high heat. Cook and stir sweet pepper and onion for 3 minutes. Add corn and chile peppers; cook and stir for 2 more minutes. Remove from heat; cool slightly.

2 Meanwhile, in a large bowl stir together cornmeal, flour, baking powder, sugar, baking soda, and salt. In another bowl, stir together the buttermilk, eggs, and the 2 tablespoons melted margarine or butter. Add the buttermilk mixture all at once to flour mixture. Stir just until moistened (batter should be lumpy). Fold in the corn mixture and cheese. Spoon batter into prepared pan. Bake for 20 to 25 minutes or until golden. Serve warm.

Nutrition facts per serving: 119 cal., 4 g total fat (1 g sat. fat), 27 mg chol., 182 mg sodium, 17 g carbo., 1 g fiber, 4 g pro.

Chile and Cheese Corn Muffins: Prepare as above, except spoon batter into 18 greased or paper-lined 2½-inch muffin cups. Bake in a 425°F oven for about 20 minutes or until muffins are golden. Cool in muffin cups on a wire rack for 5 minutes. Remove the muffins from the muffin cups; serve warm. If desired, place muffins in an airtight freezer container and freeze for up to 3 months.

easy HERB FOCACCIA

Focaccia (foh-KAH-chee-ah) is an Italian yeast bread usually topped with onions, herbs, olive oil, or cheese. Our easy version is made with a hot roll mix. Serve it with pasta or enjoy a slice as a midafternoon snack.

Prep: 20 minutes
Rise: 30 minutes
Bake: 15 minutes
Makes: 24 servings
Nonstick cooking spray

- 1 **16-ounce package hot roll mix**
- 1 **egg**
- 2 **tablespoons olive oil**
- ⅔ **cup finely chopped onion**
- 1 **teaspoon dried rosemary, crushed**
- 2 **teaspoons olive oil**

1 Spray a 15x10x1-inch baking pan or a 12- to 14-inch pizza pan with nonstick cooking spray; set aside.

2 Prepare the hot roll mix according to package directions for the basic dough, using the 1 egg and substituting the 2 tablespoons olive oil for the margarine. Knead dough; allow to rest as directed. If using the large baking pan, roll dough into a 15x10-inch rectangle and carefully transfer to prepared pan. If using the pizza pan, roll dough into a 12-inch circle and carefully transfer to prepared pan.

3 In a skillet, cook onion and rosemary in the 2 teaspoons hot olive oil until tender. With fingertips, press indentations every inch or so in dough. Top dough evenly with onion mixture. Cover and let rise in a warm place until nearly double (about 30 minutes).

4 Preheat oven to 375°F. Bake for 15 to 20 minutes or until golden. Cool for 10 minutes on a wire rack. Remove focaccia from pan; cool completely.

Nutrition facts per serving: 88 cal., 2 g total fat (0 g sat. fat), 9 mg chol., 113 mg sodium, 15 g carbo., 0 g fiber, 3 g pro.

Parmesan and Pine Nut Focaccia: Prepare focaccia as above, except omit the onion, rosemary, and 2 teaspoons olive oil. Make the indentations, then brush the dough with mixture of 1 egg white and 2 tablespoons water. Sprinkle with ¼ cup pine nuts, pressing lightly into dough. Sprinkle with 2 tablespoons grated Parmesan cheese. Bake as directed.

bacon-onion BISCUITS

Prep: 30 minutes
Bake: 25 minutes
Oven: 350°F
Makes: 12 biscuits

4 **slices bacon, chopped**

1 **large onion, chopped (1 cup)**

3 **cups all-purpose flour**

1 **tablespoon baking powder**

1 **tablespoon sugar**

¾ **teaspoon cream of tartar**

½ **teaspoon salt**

¾ **cup butter**

1 **cup milk**

❶ In a skillet, cook bacon and onion until bacon is slightly crisp and onion is tender. Drain and discard fat.

❷ In a bowl, stir together flour, baking powder, sugar, cream of tartar, and salt. Using a pastry blender, cut in butter until mixture resembles coarse crumbs. Make a well in the center of flour mixture. Combine milk and bacon mixture; add all at once to flour mixture. Using a fork, stir just until moistened.

❸ Turn dough out onto a lightly floured surface. Knead dough by folding and gently pressing dough for four to six strokes or just until dough holds together. Pat or lightly roll dough to ¾-inch thickness. Cut dough with a floured 2½-inch biscuit cutter, rerolling dough scraps as necessary. Place biscuits on a baking sheet; freeze for 1 hour. Transfer to a plastic freezer bag. Seal, label, and freeze for up to 1 month.

❹ To serve, preheat oven to 350°F. Place frozen biscuits 1 inch apart on an ungreased baking sheet. Bake for 25 minutes or until golden.

Nutrition facts per biscuit: 294 cal., 18 g total fat (10 g sat. fat), 41 mg chol., 354 mg sodium, 27 g carbo., 1 g fiber, 6 g pro.

easy PARMESAN BREADSTICKS

These versatile crispy, cheesy sticks can be served a couple of ways. Serve them restaurant-style as a meal starter. Or feature them alongside soup or salad.

Prep: 15 minutes
Bake: 10 minutes
Oven: 375°F
Makes: 6 servings

½ **of a 12-ounce loaf baguette-style French bread (halve bread loaf crosswise)**

Nonstick cooking spray

¼ **cup olive oil**

6 **tablespoons grated or finely shredded Parmesan cheese**

Purchased marinara sauce, warmed, and/or flavored oils (such as lemon-, basil-, or garlic-flavored)

1 Preheat oven to 375°F. Cut bread lengthwise into quarters; cut into ¼- to ½-inch-wide strips. (Cut bread so there is crust on each strip.)

2 Line a 15×10×1-inch baking pan with foil; lightly coat foil with nonstick cooking spray. Arrange bread strips in a single layer; drizzle with oil. Using a spatula or tongs, carefully turn breadsticks to coat with oil. Sprinkle with Parmesan cheese.

3 Bake for 10 to 12 minutes or until browned and crisp. Serve with marinara sauce and/or flavored oils.

Nutrition facts per serving: 219 cal., 13 g total fat (3 g sat. fat), 4 mg chol., 539 mg sodium, 20 g carbo., 2 g fiber, 5 g pro.

green ONION PARKER HOUSE BISCUITS

Refrigerated biscuit dough and softened herb-blend cheese make these biscuits so quick to prepare, you can serve them even when your schedule is at its most hectic.

Prep: 10 minutes
Bake: 8 minutes
Oven: 400°F
Makes: 10 biscuits

1 **5.2-ounce container Boursin cheese with garlic and herb**

¼ **cup sliced green onions**

1 **12-ounce package (10) refrigerated biscuits**

1 **egg yolk**

1 **tablespoon water**

2 **tablespoons grated Parmesan cheese**

   Sliced green onions

1 Preheat oven to 400°F. In a small bowl, stir together Boursin cheese and the ¼ cup green onions. Set aside.

2 Unwrap biscuits. Using your fingers, gently split the biscuits horizontally. Place the biscuit bottoms on a greased cookie sheet. Spread about 1 tablespoon of the cheese mixture over each biscuit bottom. Replace biscuit tops.

3 In a small bowl, use a fork to beat together egg yolk and the water. Brush biscuit tops with egg yolk mixture. Sprinkle with Parmesan cheese and additional sliced green onions. Bake for 8 to 10 minutes or until golden brown. Serve warm.

Nutrition facts per biscuit: 149 cal., 8 g total fat (5 g sat. fat), 23 mg chol., 394 mg sodium, 16 g carbo., 0 g fiber, 4 g pro.

super
SIDE DISHES

Orzo-Broccoli Pilaf, *recipe page 220*

shredded HASH BROWNS

If you like, use frozen chopped onion to shorten preparation time.

Start to Finish: 25 minutes
Makes: 2 or 3 servings

3 or 4 small russet or white potatoes (about 12 ounces total)

¼ cup finely chopped onion

1 small fresh jalapeño chile pepper, banana pepper, or Anaheim chile pepper, seeded and chopped (optional)

¼ teaspoon salt

⅛ teaspoon coarsely ground black pepper

2 tablespoons butter, cooking oil, or margarine

Fresh sage leaves (optional)

1 Peel potatoes and coarsely shred using the coarsest side of the shredder (you should have about 2 cups shredded potatoes). Rinse shredded potatoes in a colander; drain well and pat dry with paper towels. In a medium bowl, combine shredded potatoes, onion, chile pepper (if desired), salt, and black pepper.

2 In a large nonstick skillet, melt butter over medium heat. Carefully add potato mixture, pressing into an even pancakelike round (7 to 8 inches in diameter). Using a spatula, press potato mixture firmly. Cover and cook over medium heat for about 8 minutes or until golden brown. Check occasionally and reduce heat, if necessary, to prevent overbrowning.

3 Using two spatulas or a spatula and fork, turn the hash browns. (If you're not sure you can turn in a single flip, cut into quarters and turn by sections.) Cook, uncovered, for 5 to 7 minutes more or until golden brown and crisp. Remove from skillet; cut into wedges. If desired, garnish with fresh sage.

Nutrition facts per serving: 168 cal., 9 g total fat (1 g sat. fat), 0 mg chol., 197 mg sodium, 19 g carbo., 2 g fiber, 3 g pro.

herbed POTATO WEDGES

You can serve these tasty potato wedges as a snack or a side dish with flavored sour cream, ketchup, or both. No matter how you serve them, your kids will eat them up.

Prep: 15 minutes
Bake: 15 minutes
Oven: 425°F
Makes: 8 servings

2 **teaspoons olive oil**

2 **teaspoons balsamic vinegar**

1 **tablespoon grated Parmesan cheese**

1 **tablespoon fine dry bread crumbs**

½ **teaspoon dried Italian seasoning**

⅛ **teaspoon ground black pepper**

  Nonstick cooking spray

2 **medium baking potatoes**

½ **cup light dairy sour cream**

1 **tablespoon snipped fresh chives**

¼ **teaspoon garlic powder**

1 Preheat oven to 425°F. In a small bowl or custard cup, combine olive oil and balsamic vinegar. In another small bowl, combine Parmesan cheese, bread crumbs, Italian seasoning, and pepper.

2 Lightly coat a foil-lined baking sheet with nonstick cooking spray. Cut the potatoes in half lengthwise, then cut each half lengthwise into 4 wedges. Arrange potato wedges skin side down on the prepared baking sheet so they don't touch. Brush with olive oil mixture and coat with Parmesan cheese mixture.

3 Bake for 15 to 20 minutes or until potatoes are tender and edges are crisp.

4 Meanwhile, in a small bowl combine sour cream, chives, and garlic powder. Serve warm potatoes with flavored sour cream mixture.

Nutrition facts per serving: 79 cal., 3 g total fat (1 g sat. fat), 5 mg chol., 43 mg sodium, 11 g carbo., 1 g fiber, 3 g pro.

pesto POTATOES

A surefire dinner favorite, these mashed potatoes are lightened with reduced-fat cream cheese, skim milk, and a homemade, lower-fat pesto featuring basil and spinach.

Start to Finish: 35 minutes
Makes: 8 (¾-cup) servings

2 **pounds medium yellow-flesh potatoes, such as Yukon gold**

½ **of an 8-ounce package fat-free cream cheese**

Salt

Ground black pepper

2 **to 3 tablespoons skim milk**

8 **teaspoons Pesto***

1 Peel and quarter potatoes. Cook, covered, in a small amount of boiling lightly salted water for 15 to 20 minutes or until tender; drain. Mash with a potato masher or an electric mixer on low speed. Add cream cheese. Season to taste with salt and pepper. Gradually beat in enough milk to make potatoes light and fluffy. Top each serving with 1 teaspoon Pesto.

*Pesto: In a food processor bowl, combine 1 cup firmly packed fresh basil leaves; ½ cup torn fresh spinach; ¼ cup grated Parmesan cheese; ¼ cup pine nuts or almonds; 2 cloves garlic, quartered; and, if desired, ¼ teaspoon salt. Cover and process with several on-off turns until a paste forms, stopping the machine several times and scraping down the sides. With machine running, gradually add 2 tablespoons olive oil or cooking oil and 2 tablespoons water. Process to the consistency of soft butter. Cover and chill for up to 2 days or freeze for up to 1 month. Makes about ½ cup.

Nutrition facts per serving: 134 cal., 2 g total fat (1 g sat. fat), 3 mg chol., 45 mg sodium, 24 g carbo., 2 g fiber, 5 g pro.

cheddar-polenta PUFF

With an airy, soufflé-like texture, this side dish works as well for dinner as it does for brunch. Extra-sharp cheddar cheese gives an extra-rich flavor to this puff.

Prep: 40 minutes
Bake: 25 minutes
Makes: 4 servings

- 4 **egg whites**
- 1½ **cups fat-free milk**
- 2 **tablespoons finely chopped red sweet pepper**
- 1 **tablespoon thinly sliced green onion**
- ¼ **teaspoon salt**
- ⅛ **teaspoon crushed red pepper**
- ⅓ **cup cornmeal**
- 1 **egg yolk, slightly beaten**
- ¼ **cup grated Parmesan cheese**
- ¼ **cup shredded extra-sharp cheddar cheese (1 ounce)***
  Nonstick cooking spray

1 Preheat oven to 375°F. Allow egg whites to stand at room temperature for 30 minutes. Meanwhile, in a large heavy saucepan combine milk, sweet pepper, green onion, salt, and red pepper. Cook and stir over medium heat until mixture just begins to bubble. Slowly add cornmeal, stirring constantly. Cook and stir over medium heat for about 5 minutes or until mixture begins to thicken. Remove from heat. Stir half of the cornmeal mixture into the egg yolk. Return mixture to the saucepan. Stir in Parmesan cheese and cheddar cheese until melted.

2 Lightly spray a 1½-quart soufflé dish with nonstick cooking spray; set aside. In a large mixing bowl beat egg whites with an electric mixer on medium to high speed until stiff peaks form (tips stand straight). Gently fold about half of the beaten egg whites into the cheese mixture. Gradually pour cheese mixture over remaining beaten egg whites, folding to combine. Pour into prepared soufflé dish.

3 Bake for about 25 minutes or until a knife inserted in center comes out clean and top is golden brown. Serve immediately.

Nutrition facts per serving: 168 cal., 6 g total fat (4 g sat. fat), 69 mg chol., 397 mg sodium, 14 g carbo., 1 g fiber, 13 g pro.

*Note: This recipe calls for regular cheddar cheese—not reduced-fat cheddar. The baking time may cause reduced-fat cheese to toughen.

orzo-broccoli PILAF

Orzo is a tiny, rice-shaped pasta, larger than a grain of rice but slightly smaller than a pine nut. It is a great substitute for rice in this vegetable-filled pilaf.

Prep: 20 minutes
Cook: 15 minutes
Stand: 5 minutes
Makes: 6 (⅔-cup) servings

2 **teaspoons olive oil**

1 **cup sliced fresh mushrooms**

½ **cup chopped onion**

⅔ **cup orzo**

1 **14.5-ounce can reduced-sodium chicken broth**

½ **cup shredded carrot**

1 **teaspoon dried marjoram, crushed**

⅛ **teaspoon ground black pepper**

2 **cups small broccoli florets**

❶ In a large saucepan, heat olive oil over medium-high heat. Cook and stir the mushrooms and onion in hot oil until onion is tender. Stir in the orzo. Cook and stir for about 2 minutes more or until orzo is lightly browned. Remove from heat.

❷ Carefully stir in the chicken broth, carrot, marjoram, and pepper. Bring to boiling; reduce heat. Simmer, covered, for about 15 minutes or until orzo is tender but still firm. Remove saucepan from heat; stir in broccoli. Let stand, covered, for 5 minutes.

Nutrition facts per serving: 113 cal., 2 g total fat (0 g sat. fat), 0 mg chol., 209 mg sodium, 19 g carbo., 2 g fiber, 4 g pro.

lemon-pepper BABY BROCCOLI

Baby broccoli, called broccolini, is a cross between broccoli and Chinese kale. Because of its tender stem, it cooks quickly.

Start to Finish: 20 minutes
Makes: 8 servings

1 cup reduced-sodium chicken broth

1 tablespoon snipped fresh dill

2 teaspoons finely shredded lemon peel

1 teaspoon olive oil

½ teaspoon coarse salt

⅛ teaspoon crushed red pepper

⅛ teaspoon ground black pepper

1 pound baby broccoli or broccoli rabe

2 tablespoons butter

Lemon halves or slices (optional)

1 In a large skillet, combine chicken broth, dill, lemon peel, olive oil, coarse salt, crushed red pepper, and black pepper. Bring to boiling; reduce heat. Cover and simmer for 5 minutes.

2 Add broccoli and butter to skillet. Cover and cook over medium heat for 6 to 8 minutes or until broccoli is tender. If desired, drain. Transfer broccoli mixture to a serving bowl. If desired, garnish with lemon halves or slices.

Nutrition facts per serving: 47 cal., 3 g total fat (2 g sat. fat), 8 mg chol., 489 mg sodium, 4 g carbo., 2 g fiber, 2 g pro.

asparagus AND ROASTED PEPPERS

If you grow your own sweet peppers, you can roast them yourself. However, convenient roasted peppers from a jar provide a jump-start on this dish. Here, they are pureed into a colorful sauce for asparagus or broccoli.

Start to Finish: 25 minutes
Makes: 4 servings

½ of a 7.25-ounce jar (about ½ cup) roasted red sweet peppers, drained

¼ cup water

1 teaspoon snipped fresh thyme or savory or ¼ teaspoon dried thyme or savory, crushed

1 teaspoon lemon juice

½ teaspoon cornstarch

¼ teaspoon instant chicken bouillon granules

⅛ teaspoon ground black pepper

12 ounces asparagus or broccoli, cut lengthwise into spears

1 For sauce, in a blender container or food processor bowl, combine the sweet peppers, water, thyme or savory, lemon juice, cornstarch, bouillon granules, and black pepper. Cover and blend or process until smooth. Pour into a small saucepan. Cook and stir until thickened and bubbly. Cook and stir for 2 minutes more. Cover and keep warm.

2 In a large saucepan, cook the asparagus, covered, in a small amount of boiling water for 4 to 6 minutes or until crisp-tender. (Or, cook broccoli for 8 to 10 minutes or until crisp-tender.) Drain well. To serve, spoon the sauce over the asparagus or broccoli.

Nutrition facts per serving (with 2 tablespoons sauce): 27 cal., 0 g total fat (0 g sat. fat), 0 mg chol., 58 mg sodium, 5 g carbo., 2 g fiber, 2 g pro.

One Sweet Pepper

Roasting sweet peppers draws out their natural sweetness and flavor. To roast the peppers, cut them into quarters. Remove stems, membranes, and seeds. Place the pepper pieces, cut side down, on a foil-lined baking sheet. Bake in a 425°F oven for 20 to 25 minutes or until skins are bubbly and very dark. Wrap pepper pieces tightly in foil and let stand for 10 to 15 minutes or until cool enough to handle. Using a paring knife, pull the skin off gently. Use the peppers as directed in recipes, or cut into strips and toss with salads, layer on sandwiches, or stir into vegetable dishes.

caramelized BRUSSELS SPROUTS

Prep: 15 minutes
Cook: 21 minutes
Makes: 8 servings

**5 cups small, firm fresh Brussels
    sprouts (about 1½ pounds)**

¼ cup sugar

2 tablespoons butter

¼ cup red wine vinegar

⅓ cup water

½ teaspoon salt

1 Prepare the Brussels sprouts by peeling off two or three of the dark outer leaves from each Brussels sprout; trim stem ends.

2 In a large skillet, heat sugar over medium-high heat until it begins to melt, shaking pan occasionally to heat sugar evenly. Once sugar starts to melt, reduce heat and cook until sugar begins to turn brown. Add butter; stir until melted. Add vinegar. Cook and stir for 1 minute.

3 Carefully add the water and salt. Bring to boiling; add Brussels sprouts. Return to boiling; reduce heat. Simmer, covered, for 6 minutes.

4 Uncover and cook for about 15 minutes more or until most of the liquid has been absorbed and the sprouts are coated with a golden glaze, gently stirring occasionally.

Nutrition facts per serving: 76 cal., 3 g total fat (2 g sat. fat), 8 mg chol., 155 mg sodium, 11 g carbo., 2 g fiber, 2 g pro.

sautéed SPINACH WITH BACON AND MUSTARD

Start to Finish: 15 minutes
Makes: 4 to 6 servings

4 slices bacon, cut into 1-inch pieces

2 10-ounce bags prewashed spinach

1 tablespoon butter

1 tablespoon Dijon-style mustard

¼ teaspoon crushed red pepper

1 In a very large skillet, cook bacon over medium heat until crisp. Drain bacon on paper towels, reserving 1 tablespoon drippings in skillet. Gradually add spinach to skillet, stirring frequently with metal tongs. Cook for 2 to 3 minutes or until spinach is just wilted. Transfer spinach from skillet to a colander; hold over sink and press lightly with the back of a spoon to drain.

2 In the same skillet, melt butter over medium heat; stir in mustard and crushed red pepper. Add drained spinach; toss to coat. Reheat spinach if necessary. Top with bacon. Serve immediately.

Nutrition facts per serving: 135 cal., 11 g total fat (4 g sat. fat), 18 mg chol., 340 mg sodium, 5 g carbo., 3 g fiber, 7 g pro.

roasted SUCCOTASH

Put away your saucepan! This colorful lima bean, corn, and red pepper succotash is prepared in the oven. Just combine the ingredients in the pan, bake, and finish with a light sprinkling of fresh cilantro.

Prep: 15 minutes
Bake: 25 minutes
Makes: 6 (½-cup) servings

- 1 **10-ounce package frozen baby lima beans**
- 1½ **cups fresh or frozen whole kernel corn**
- 1½ **cups finely chopped red sweet pepper**
- 1 **cup chopped onion**
- 1 **tablespoon olive oil**
- 1 **teaspoon ground cumin**
- ¼ **teaspoon salt**
- ⅛ **to ¼ teaspoon crushed red pepper**
- 1 **to 2 tablespoons snipped cilantro**

1 Preheat oven to 400°F. In a 15x10x1-inch baking pan, combine lima beans, corn, sweet pepper, onion, olive oil, cumin, salt, and red pepper.

2 Bake for about 25 minutes or until vegetables are tender and lightly browned, stirring after 15 minutes. To serve, sprinkle with cilantro.

Nutrition facts per serving: 210 cal., 3 g total fat (1 g sat. fat), 0 mg chol., 100 mg sodium, 37 g carbo., 5 g fiber, 11 g pro.

orange-ginger CARROTS

Consider keeping fresh ginger on hand to add zesty flavor to vegetables. The knobby tan root stays fresh in the refrigerator for at least a week. It also can be frozen for up to 2 months.

Start to Finish: 10 minutes
Makes: 4 (¾-cup) servings

- 1 **16-ounce package peeled baby carrots**
- 2 **tablespoons orange juice**
- 1 **tablespoon honey**
- ½ **teaspoon grated fresh ginger**
- 1 **tablespoon snipped fresh parsley**
- **Finely shredded orange peel (optional)**

1 In a large saucepan, cook the carrots, covered, in a small amount of boiling water for 3 to 5 minutes or until crisp-tender. Drain well.

2 Meanwhile, in a small bowl stir together the orange juice, honey, and ginger; drizzle over warm carrots. Toss to coat. To serve, sprinkle with parsley and, if desired, orange peel.

Nutrition facts per serving: 67 cal., 0 g total fat (0 g sat. fat), 0 mg chol., 70 mg sodium, 16 g carbo., 4 g fiber, 1 g pro.

grapefruit-avocado SALAD

Start to Finish: 15 minutes
Makes: 6 servings

4 **cups packaged fresh baby spinach**

1 **grapefruit, peeled and sectioned**

1 **small avocado, halved, pitted, peeled, and sliced**

1 **cup canned sliced beets**

1 **tablespoon sliced almonds, toasted**

Orange Vinaigrette*

1 Divide spinach among four salad plates. Arrange grapefruit sections, avocado slices, and beets on spinach. Top with almonds. Drizzle with Orange Vinaigrette.

***Orange Vinaigrette:** In a screw-top jar, combine 1 teaspoon finely shredded orange peel, ⅓ cup orange juice, 2 teaspoons red wine vinegar, 2 teaspoons salad oil, ⅛ teaspoon salt, and pinch ground black pepper. Cover and shake well.

Nutrition facts per serving: 106 cal., 7 g total fat (1 g sat. fat), 0 mg chol., 122 mg sodium, 11 g carbo., 4 g fiber, 2 g pro.

greek VEGETABLE SALAD

This healthful Greek-inspired salad of tomatoes, cucumber, sweet pepper, and feta cheese is lightly dressed in an herb vinaigrette.

Start to Finish: 30 minutes
Makes: 8 servings

- 2 **cups chopped tomatoes**
- 1 **cup chopped cucumber**
- ½ **cup chopped yellow, red, or green sweet pepper**
- ¼ **cup chopped red onion**
- 1½ **teaspoons snipped fresh thyme or ½ teaspoon dried thyme, crushed**
- 1 **teaspoon snipped fresh oregano or ¼ teaspoon dried oregano, crushed**
- 2 **tablespoons white balsamic vinegar or regular balsamic vinegar**
- 2 **tablespoons olive oil**
  Leaf lettuce (optional)
- ½ **cup crumbled feta cheese (2 ounces)**

❶ In a large bowl, combine tomatoes, cucumber, sweet pepper, red onion, thyme, and oregano. For dressing, in a small bowl, whisk together balsamic vinegar and olive oil. Pour dressing over vegetable mixture. Toss gently to coat.

❷ If desired, line a serving bowl with lettuce; spoon in vegetable mixture. Sprinkle with feta cheese.

Nutrition facts per serving: 65 cal., 5 g total fat (1 g sat. fat), 3 mg chol., 120 mg sodium, 4 g carbo., 1 g fiber, 2 g pro.

pear-walnut SALAD WITH DIJON VINAIGRETTE

Start to Finish: 20 minutes
Makes: 4 servings

2   medium ripe pears, cored and thinly sliced lengthwise

Dijon Vinaigrette*

1   medium head Boston or Bibb lettuce

2   ounces Gorgonzola or blue cheese, cut into wedges

¼   cup walnut pieces, toasted

1   large yellow or red tomato, seeded and chopped

1 In a medium bowl, toss pear slices with ⅓ cup of the Dijon Vinaigrette.

2 To serve, line four salad plates or bowls with lettuce leaves. Top with pear mixture. Top each serving with cheese, walnuts, and tomato. Drizzle with remaining Dijon Vinaigrette.

*Dijon Vinaigrette: In a screw-top jar, combine ½ cup olive oil; ¼ cup white wine vinegar; 1 tablespoon sugar; 1 tablespoon Dijon-style mustard; 1 clove garlic, minced; ¼ teaspoon salt; and ¼ teaspoon ground black pepper. Cover and shake well. Serve immediately or store in refrigerator for up to 1 week. Stir just before serving. Makes about 1 cup.

Nutrition facts per serving: 419 cal., 36 g total fat (7 g sat. fat), 11 mg chol., 414 mg sodium, 20 g carbo., 4 g fiber, 6 g pro.

metric information

The charts on this page provide a guide for converting measurements from the U.S. customary system, which is used throughout this book, to the metric system.

PRODUCT DIFFERENCES

Most of the ingredients called for in the recipes in this book are available in most countries. However, some are known by different names. Here are some common American ingredients and their possible counterparts:

- Sugar (white) is granulated, fine granulated, or castor sugar.
- Powdered sugar is icing sugar.
- All-purpose flour is enriched, bleached, or unbleached white household flour. When self-rising flour is used in place of all-purpose flour in a recipe that calls for leavening, omit the leavening agent (baking soda or baking powder) and salt.
- Light-colored corn syrup is golden syrup.
- Cornstarch is cornflour.
- Baking soda is bicarbonate of soda.
- Vanilla or vanilla extract is vanilla essence.
- Green, red, or yellow sweet peppers are capsicums or bell peppers.
- Golden raisins are sultanas.

VOLUME AND WEIGHT

The United States traditionally uses cup measures for liquid and solid ingredients. The chart, top right, shows the approximate imperial and metric equivalents. If you are accustomed to weighing solid ingredients, the following approximate equivalents will be helpful.

- 1 cup butter, castor sugar, or rice = 8 ounces = $\frac{1}{2}$ pound = 250 grams
- 1 cup flour = 4 ounces = $\frac{1}{4}$ pound = 125 grams
- 1 cup icing sugar = 5 ounces = 150 grams

Canadian and U.S. volume for a cup measure is 8 fluid ounces (237 ml), but the standard metric equivalent is 250 ml.

1 British imperial cup is 10 fluid ounces.

In Australia, 1 tablespoon equals 20 ml, and there are 4 teaspoons in the Australian tablespoon.

Spoon measures are used for smaller amounts of ingredients. Although the size of the tablespoon varies slightly in different countries, for practical purposes and for recipes in this book, a straight substitution is all that's necessary. Measurements made using cups or spoons always should be level unless stated otherwise.

COMMON WEIGHT RANGE REPLACEMENTS

Imperial / U.S.	Metric
$\frac{1}{2}$ ounce	15 g
1 ounce	25 g or 30 g
4 ounces ($\frac{1}{4}$ pound)	115 g or 125 g
8 ounces ($\frac{1}{2}$ pound)	225 g or 250 g
16 ounces (1 pound)	450 g or 500 g
$1\frac{1}{4}$ pounds	625 g
$1\frac{1}{2}$ pounds	750 g
2 pounds or $2\frac{1}{4}$ pounds	1,000 g or 1 Kg

OVEN TEMPERATURE EQUIVALENTS

Fahrenheit Setting	Celsius Setting*	Gas Setting
300°F	150°C	Gas Mark 2 (very low)
325°F	160°C	Gas Mark 3 (low)
350°F	180°C	Gas Mark 4 (moderate)
375°F	190°C	Gas Mark 5 (moderate)
400°F	200°C	Gas Mark 6 (hot)
425°F	220°C	Gas Mark 7 (hot)
450°F	230°C	Gas Mark 8 (very hot)
475°F	240°C	Gas Mark 9 (very hot)
500°F	260°C	Gas Mark 10 (extremely hot)
Broil	Broil	Grill

*Electric and gas ovens may be calibrated using Celsius. However, for an electric oven, increase Celsius setting 10 to 20 degrees when cooking above 160°C. For convection or forced air ovens (gas or electric), lower the temperature setting 25°F/10°C when cooking at all heat levels.

BAKING PAN SIZES

Imperial / U.S.	Metric
9×1$\frac{1}{2}$-inch round cake pan	22- or 23×4-cm (1.5 L)
9×1$\frac{1}{2}$-inch pie plate	22- or 23×4-cm (1 L)
8×8×2-inch square cake pan	20×5-cm (2 L)
9×9×2-inch square cake pan	22- or 23×4.5-cm (2.5 L)
11×7×1$\frac{1}{2}$-inch baking pan	28×17×4-cm (2 L)
2-quart rectangular baking pan	30×19×4.5-cm (3 L)
13×9×2-inch baking pan	34×22×4.5-cm (3.5 L)
15×10×1-inch jelly roll pan	40×25×2-cm
9×5×3-inch loaf pan	23×13×8-cm (2 L)
2-quart casserole	2 L

U.S. / STANDARD METRIC EQUIVALENTS

$\frac{1}{8}$ teaspoon = 0.5 ml	$\frac{1}{3}$ cup = 3 fluid ounces = 75 ml
$\frac{1}{4}$ teaspoon = 1 ml	$\frac{1}{2}$ cup = 4 fluid ounces = 125 ml
$\frac{1}{2}$ teaspoon = 2 ml	$\frac{1}{3}$ cup = 5 fluid ounces = 150 ml
1 teaspoon = 5 ml	$\frac{3}{4}$ cup = 6 fluid ounces = 175 ml
1 tablespoon = 15 ml	1 cup = 8 fluid ounces = 250 ml
2 tablespoons = 25 ml	2 cups = 1 pint = 500 ml
$\frac{1}{4}$ cup = 2 fluid ounces = 50 ml	1 quart = 1 liter

index

Note: *Italicized* page references indicate photographs.